Soul Dog

"*Soul Dog* is a very thought-provoking book. Steeped in science and heart, Ms. Mannes passionately shares her own experiences with Brio. This book opens the door for wide-ranging musings about what dogs can teach us if we open our minds and hearts."

MARC BEKOFF, AUTHOR OF
CANINE CONFIDENTIAL: WHY DOGS DO WHAT THEY DO

"Do you have a dog and wonder about your relationship? Then this is a must-read. A touching, insightful, and thought-provoking book that compels you to look at your animals in a new way. It is a wonderful example of just how deep and mutually enriching the dog-human relationship can be."

DIANE BUDD, ANIMAL COMMUNICATOR AND HEALER
AND AUTHOR OF *ENERGY MEDICINE FOR ANIMALS*

"Elena Mannes writes eloquently of her unfolding journey of awareness with soul dog Brio. With gentle nudges and congenial canine humor, Brio guides Mannes through the mysteries of animal communication and ultimately helps her awaken to the magic that occurs when we learn to trust and listen to the truth of our deeper self."

DAWN BAUMANN BRUNKE, AUTHOR OF *SHAPESHIFTING WITH
OUR ANIMAL COMPANIONS, DREAMING WITH POLAR BEARS,*
AND *ANIMAL VOICES, ANIMAL GUIDES*

"Elena and Brio's soul story showcases the precious trans-species adoration and communication in life and the afterlife between a woman and her dog. Discovering Brio's creative and original mind, Mannes's own testimony, both reflective and humorous, weaves science and personal experience into a kind of Tao of dog. She shows that sentient animal kin are teaching humans how to sit, walk, stay, and lie down in reciprocal respect, love, and joy. This book sparkles with delight."

ZOHARA M. HIERONIMUS, D.H.L., AUTHOR OF
WHITE SPIRIT ANIMALS: PROPHETS OF CHANGE

"Hidden in the fabric of a curly coat, Elena Mannes discovers a real, in-the-flesh angel whom she comes to know as her soul dog, Brio. She teaches us that a soul dog connects us with our own all-knowing soul, the indestructible force of God that lives within us and within the animals that we may take for granted. This brave author beautifully balances incredibly precise messages from animal communicators and psychics with scientific studies all directed at the same discovery—we are more connected than we might think. May every reader be inspired to listen to the far-reaching wisdom of a trusted pet and be blessed to have your heart blown open by the healing power of their unconditional, and forever, love."

BELINDA J. WOMACK, AUTHOR OF *LESSONS FROM THE TWELVE
ARCHANGELS: DIVINE INTERVENTION IN DAILY LIFE*

Soul Dog

A Journey into the
Spiritual Life of Animals

ELENA MANNES

Bear & Company
Rochester, Vermont

Bear & Company
One Park Street
Rochester, Vermont 05767
www.BearandCompanyBooks.com

Bear & Company is a division of Inner Traditions International

Library of Congress Cataloging-in-Publication Data

Names: Mannes, Elena, author.
Title: Soul dog : a journey into the spiritual life of animals / Elena Mannes.
Description: Rochester, Vermont : Bear & Company, [2018] | Includes
    bibliographical references and index.
Identifiers: LCCN 2018014302 (print) | LCCN 2018021817 (ebook) |
    ISBN 9781591433262 (paperback) | ISBN 9781591433279 (ebook)
Subjects: LCSH: Dogs—Anecdotes. | Dogs—Psychology—Anecdotes. |
    Human-animal communication.
Classification: LCC SF426.2 .M353 2018 (print) | LCC SF426.2 (ebook) |
    DDC 636.7—dc23
LC record available at https://lccn.loc.gov/2018014302

Printed and bound in Canada by Friesens Corporation

10   9   8   7   6   5   4   3   2

Text design by Priscilla H. Baker and layout by Virginia Scott Bowman
This book was typeset in Garamond Premier Pro with Hypatia Sans and Jelytta
used as display typefaces

The Hafiz verse on the facing page is from the unpublished Hafiz work of Daniel Ladinsky, copyright 2007, and used with permission.
"Saints Bowing in the Mountains," on page 146, is from *I Heard God Laughing* by Daniel Ladinsky, copyright 1996, and used with permission.

To send correspondence to the author of this book, mail a first-class letter to the author c/o Inner Traditions • Bear & Company, One Park Street, Rochester, VT 05767, and we will forward the communication, or contact the author directly at **http://mannesproductions.com**.

To Brio

～⁓～

Yours was the heart I cared most for in this world,

and yours was the heart that cared most for me.

HAFIZ

Contents

Foreword

WHAT A WONDROUS JOURNEY OF DISCOVERY and fulfillment does
Elena Mannes tell us about in this deeply moving tale of her relationship
with the brilliant, elegant, wise, and loving poodle Brio, her "soul dog"!
She falls in love with him and becomes deeply entangled for as many
years as possible in the all-too-short life span of our canine friends. He
becomes not only best friend and soul mate but even a kind of Yoda-like
spiritual mentor, causing a down-to-earth, practical, hard-nosed journalist and documentarian to go deep within herself while also expanding
her investigations into the far-out realms of "mind" or "spiritual" science.
This most subtle area of human scientific exploration is called "inner science" in India and was highly developed there in classical times. It was
considered the peerless queen of all sciences, in contrast with the mostly
externally oriented Euro-American material sciences.

Ms. Mannes brings to life the extraordinary persona of Brio, the
soul dog, in his many graceful manifestations and takes us with her
on her own inner journey of finding her deeper humanity by realizing
her vitally enriching interconnectedness with the sparkling intelligence
of especially that dog, and through him the multifarious world of all
conscious animals. Some of the phenomena she experiences are nothing
short of miraculous, yet her deep engagement and vivid description has
a powerful ring of authenticity that is utterly convincing.

In spite of her own starting point of having been indoctrinated in the scientific materialism that is the orthodoxy of our twentieth-century American culture, Ms. Mannes follows her intuitive heart under the psychic guidance of the soul dog Brio, while using her relentlessly critical, investigative journalistic methodology to explore the realm of animal communication and the history of the one-hundred-thousand-year-old human-dog relationship. She consults in careful detail all kinds of conventional and unconventional experts and chronicles in an intricate tapestry of anecdotes the amazing world of human-canine interactions in our contemporary hi-tech but fragmented world of the information age.

After she loses the physical presence of Brio, due to the disparities in human and canine life spans, she tells us movingly of her desolation at his departure and her deep grieving. She then turns to a study of the afterlife realm, revealing how intensely people are still preoccupied with it, in spite of the authoritative assurances we are given by scientific materialists that only the Big Nothing awaits both humans and animals. Rising above her youthful intimidation by this dominant materialist culture, she explores the most advanced researches into the biological discovery of morphic resonance of nonverbal sentient communication, into the "paranormal" of special mental abilities such as telepathy and clairvoyance, and into the extensive mass of anecdotal data about the vivid memories of previous lives in people from a wide variety of cultures.

Eventually she gains a sense of the enduring presence of her soul dog, beyond the seemingly ineluctable barriers of space and time, and leaves us with an inspiring example of a heroic woman with her mind open to the joy of interconnectedness with all living beings, her heart buoyant with a sense of oneness with the basic goodness of life as mediated by Brio, her by now angelic soul dog, and her feet firmly on the ground of this world of wondrous possibility.

At one point Ms. Mannes interviews me about *The Great Book of Natural Liberation Through Understanding in the Between* (popularly misnamed *The Tibetan Book of the Dead*), and she respectfully and accurately reports on some of the findings of the Indian and Tibetan inner scientists and the psychonauts who traveled these realms and reported on them long ago to their Sanskrit and Tibetan refined civilization. And I was pleased that she felt at home with the Tibetan Buddhist sense that dogs, in particular among the animals, are the emanations (as they describe incarnations) of a very advanced archangelic "enlightenment hero" (bodhisattva) named Maitreya, who is expected to grace the planet in Buddha-form many thousands of years in the future. In the meantime, he presents himself to anxious, frightened, overburdened, and lonely humans as loyal, devoted, intelligent, and gentle dogs who become their masters' living doorways to the basic goodness of the real world, the generosity of nature, and the joy of warmhearted openness to all life.

It is my honor and pleasure to greet this fine work and invite you all to enjoy its magical gifts.

ROBERT A. F. THURMAN

ROBERT A. F. THURMAN, a recognized worldwide authority on religion and spirituality, holds the first endowed chair in Buddhist studies in the West, the Jey Tsong Khapa Chair in Indo-Tibetan Buddhist Studies at Columbia University. He is president of Tibet House U.S., a nonprofit organization dedicated to the preservation and promotion of Tibetan culture. The author of many scholarly works and popular books, including *Infinite Life* and *Inner Revolution,* in 1997 he was named one of *Time* magazine's twenty-five most influential Americans.

PROLOGUE

An Unbroken Bond

THIS IS MUCH MORE THAN THE STORY of a special bond with a dog. Many have experienced the depth of feeling that can develop between us and our four-legged best friends. What makes this story unique is that my search for a lasting and meaningful connection led me down a path that crossed over the boundaries of reason and concrete reality into the realm of the invisible. My dog Brio inspired me—a born skeptic—to investigate the paranormal. In doing so, I discovered that there is much more to heaven and earth than I had ever dreamed of as a fact-driven investigative journalist. Once we become open to new possibilities, we become open to a new world.

I grew up on pragmatism and logic based on my parents' teachings. Trained as a reporter, I built my career in television journalism, and lived my life bound by reason and fact. I saw myself as a questioning rationalist and still do, in many respects—at least as I function in the everyday world. But I stepped beyond my "comfortable" world in which everything had its place and made sense, and I ventured into foreign territory.

This book is about taking that step.

No doubt many people who develop particularly close relationships with dogs do describe the connection as remarkable. But surely a far fewer number embark on the kind of quest I undertook; they generally don't question the nature of their pet's spiritual origins. I came to contemplate the possibility of a wordless language between species. Moreover, I considered that such a conversation could take place across time and space and even across the boundary of physical death.

I entered a world of animal communicators, psychics, and mediums. In the beginning I would tell myself that it was a journalist's curious drive to investigate that led me down this road. In truth, I was fascinated. As a journalist, once I began to see evidence of a reality I had never contemplated before, there was no turning back. I had to get to the bottom of it all. Then, after the communicators and intuitives succeeded in convincing me, I began to turn my journey inward and develop my own spiritual aptitude.

Of course, I didn't come around to this new way of thinking immediately. My beginning steps were full of doubt and suspicion. But when the animal psychics and communicators began to report on their conversations with animals with startling accuracy, I had to acknowledge that whatever these people were doing, it was working.

As much as I questioned how the communicators could possibly know or hear or somehow see what my dog was "saying," I couldn't deny they had access to information I had not verbally given them, information they could not have known by ordinary means. I came to accept that something extraordinary was happening, though I could not explain how or why.

This is the story of a continuing quest, of efforts to test the communicators and psychics, to gather the experience and opinion of other dog people, including professionals. Respected trainers and handlers interviewed for the book include Carol Benjamin, Donald McCaig—border collie trainer and author—and Elizabeth Marshall Thomas, also a highly regarded trainer and author. Their insight offered invaluable perspective. Some professional handlers believe the idea of psychic communication with dogs is an insult to traditional training methods. Others are open to the possibility of an extrasensory language; some have even become committed believers. Furthermore, some scientists whom I interviewed are convinced of a canine afterlife.

I sought out other people I trusted who had especially close relationships with dogs to ask about their experiences with communication between species. I strove to understand how the psychics work, how they could possibly get accurate information over a phone line about a dog they had never seen.

The voices of the animal communicators and psychics with whom I spoke were very important. The tone and frequent beauty of their words were often as convincing as the content of what they said. It would be impossible to tell this story and convey the emotional impact of what I heard without bringing the voice of these translators as close to the reader as possible. So I have quoted them often. As a tale of an intimate relationship with a dog, this is not an uncommon story—not even as an account of personal change and even transformation through that relationship. That is something many readers experience. My adventure is unique because it is an exploration into telepathy, afterlife communication, and metaphysics—which walks all of us on the journey out of skepticism, to curiosity, to the need to believe, the need to find proof, to a crisis of faith and, finally, into a new understanding of the unbreakable bond between humans and animals.

It is one thing to call oneself an "animal lover." It is something else entirely to see a dog as an equal being, as much a teacher as a student and pet. That is one blessing that this journey has brought me: the understanding and conviction that a dog is a thinking, feeling, and yes, spiritual being. Dogs do have souls, and lives that extend beyond death's limitless horizon. Once you know this, how hard it becomes to speak of *owners* and of *pets*. How hard to think of dogs—or any animal—as creatures meant merely to obey and serve us.

From the beginning, I was not in control. I had expected a companion over whom I was master. I quickly learned that Brio, the dog who would change my life, was his own master. Our relationship was far from what I would have called *normal*. I recall what Pablo Picasso said about his dachshund, Lump: "Lump, he's not a dog, he's not a little man, he's somebody else."[1] That's what this puppy, Brio, became for me—"something else." This being, in the clothing of another species, was—is—to me, a great spirit. Our relationship exceeded all expectations. It has taken me to a place, a consciousness I could have never foreseen—one that continues to surprise and amaze me even today, long after his passing. In truth, his was the first soul I came to love.

In the course of my journey with Brio, I have moved from being someone who feared close relationships, struggled with them, to someone who bonded deeply with another creature in life and death. I have become a more loving, engaged, open person because of the rich and uncomplicated bond I shared with Brio. Our journey together transformed me entirely and seamlessly, through the power of unconditional love and a deeply instructive spiritual connection.

I understand that the bond with Brio is unbroken even in death, not figuratively or metaphorically, but with an unshakable conviction that was once incomprehensible to me. This brings me an enormous sense of peace and gratitude about my own life, its meaning, and its transitions. There is gratitude also for the fact that my need to understand "just a dog" led me to explore aspects of existence that I'd never considered. Do dogs—do all beings—have abilities to perceive that transcend the five senses? Do these "extra" senses offer ways to communicate within and between species in ways that the precepts of Western, materialistic science do not acknowledge? The seventeenth-century French philosopher and scientist René Descartes shaped centuries of modern scientific thought with his doctrine that materialism is the only explanation of reality.

According to this view, there are no *metaphysical* ("beyond the physical") truths. There is no consciousness that exists outside of or is not governed by the physical brain. Some scientists and philosophers are now questioning this view. Quantum physics, certainly, is challenging the view that everything—including our minds, our consciousness—is fundamentally physical, material. There is also a discernable shift in scientific thinking about our fellow animals. Descartes had insisted that only humans have the ability to reason and think because only humans have verbal language.

In the nineteenth century Charles Darwin opposed this belief. Darwin is often credited with having given birth to the field of animal-mind research. Darwin said, "There is no fundamental difference between man and the higher mammals in their mental faculties."[2] Today there is much new activity among scientists eager to investigate the intelligence, cognition, emotions, and communication capabilities of nonhuman animals.

As I consider these developments in the world of science, philosophy, and understanding of animals, it seems that my personal transformation coincides with a much larger shift in perception about our relationship to our fellow beings.

One might say that mine was a journey on two parallel paths: rooted in the immediate joys of life with a dog, right here in the now, the walking, the running, the tail wags, the smiles, yet simultaneously leading me down a road toward tantalizing questions about who animals are and what they tell us about who we human animals are as well. It's a journey to revel in.

Acknowledgments

THIS BOOK WAS BORN OUT OF MY OWN EXPERIENCE, yet it would have remained a mere seedling struggling to bloom without the talent and support of many people. The extent of their generosity seemed truly miraculous.

I am profoundly grateful to my wonderful agent, Jane Lahr, and her partner, Lynn DelliQuadri, of Lahr & Partners. Their efforts on behalf of *Soul Dog* have been above and beyond what any author could expect of an agent, providing faith, enthusiasm, and Jane's invaluable and profound knowledge of spiritual teachings relevant to my subject.

To Maria Cooper Janis, who introduced me to Jane, I owe a great debt of gratitude. She too helped sustain the creation of this book with her understanding of my story and my intent in working to bring it forth.

The journey that I've recounted in this book is one that I took in the company of animal communicators and psychics who became my guides and my friends; their voices are inextricably woven into the fabric of the story. They opened doors to new understanding—of our fellow beings and of myself. I am deeply grateful to Alecia Evans, Dawn Hayman, Donna Lozito, and Silvia Rossi. You know what you did.

There were many others who contributed their time and expertise by allowing me to interview them for this endeavor. I am very much in their debt. (For more information about the many contributors to this endeavor, please see the interview credits at the end of this book.)

I also thank Dr. Jennifer Chaitman, Brio's wonderful veterinarian, who gave her support and time. I'm grateful to Brio's other longtime caregivers—Stacey Baum, Sally Hastings, Jim Moran, and Micky Niego.

For their friendship, advice, and support over the years of my life with Brio and then through the writing of this book, I am so very thankful to Michael and Susan Batcheller, Susan Buckley, David Buksbaum, Bob and Arline Prince, Giuliana Robertson, and Arnulfo Vargas.

I want to thank Jamaica Burns Griffin, my editor at Inner Traditions • Bear & Company, for her hard work and valued input. I'm grateful as well for the support of the superb team at Inner Traditions. I thank Jon Graham, who championed the book; John Hays for his marketing wizardry; Manzanita Carpenter Sanz for her skill and dedication in promoting the book; and publisher Ehud Sperling for bringing this book to readers.

I am also fortunate to have received invaluable advice from Carmen and Alexandra Harra and Beverly West.

To Robert Thurman, who wrote such a beautiful and profound foreword, I give great thanks for his understanding of the book and of what our relationship with dogs and other fellow creatures truly means.

Finally and forever, thank you to Brio—my inspiration.

1

Your Name Is Brio!

HE LOOKED AT ME HEAD-ON, STRAIGHT IN THE EYE. No guilt. No fear. Just: *Here I am. You called?* On an early spring day, at a mere nine months old, there was a self-possession about him that made one take notice. I had indeed been calling him for quite some time, screaming in New York City's Central Park, convinced that I would never see him again. Now I was dripping wet. As I'd walked backward in panic, calling for him, there was suddenly no ground beneath my feet. I had stepped into the abyss—actually over the rim of a pond, fortunately not too deep. It was humiliating.

Someone I knew recognized me: "Oh my goodness, that was you! I thought a homeless person had jumped into the pond to take a bath!" she said. Then too there was the truth of the matter: I literally and figuratively had jumped off the edge into unknown territory and found myself with no ground beneath my feet. I'd wanted a dog. I hadn't expected it to be like this. It wasn't working out as planned. On this fresh cool morning, with the promise of beginnings in the air, my soaked jeans and sodden sneakers spoke more of disappointment and doubt.

There's no question that most people have an easier time connecting with their dog than I did initially. The storied bond between human and dog seemed just that to me at the time: storied, out of reach. I felt I didn't know this being who shared (sometimes invaded) my life. I'm now convinced that even if I didn't know him, Brio had known me from the start.

Since time immemorial, dogs have held the title of "man's best friend," a fitting moniker for their loyal and protective disposition toward their human companions. Researchers now believe that the dog-human relationship began tens of thousands of years ago. Genetic evidence indicates a link as long as 145,000 years ago between the wolf and a kind of wolf-dog—the ones who would go on to evolve into pure dogs. Perhaps wolves started hanging around humans to scavenge for food. Perhaps they became hunting companions. We can imagine our ancestors around a fire, sharing a meal they had secured with the help of their canine companions.

We also have archaeological evidence of the respect those ancestors felt for companions of another species. Zooarchaeologists and evolutionary biologists have found prehistoric dog burial sites. One dog skull had a mammoth bone in its mouth, indicating some kind of ritual paying homage to a hunting companion. Recently archaeologists found dogs buried twenty-five hundred years ago in ancient Ashkelon, a city half an hour from Tel Aviv. The dogs' bodies had been placed on their sides with legs flexed and tails carefully tucked around their hind legs.[1] There is also the recent finding of a fourteen-thousand-year-old burial site in Germany that featured a dog who had been buried with humans, together with evidence that the dog had been domesticated and cared for.[2]

Perhaps the early humans rejected the wolves they didn't like and accepted those they did—the ones who were easier to live with. Perhaps this kind of natural selection led to the evolution of the domesticated dog, a dog born to connect with human beings.

In truth, I had expected a connection, but not really a partnership. When I entertained the notion of getting a puppy, I had a vision of adorable cuddly standard poodles curling into my lap, allowing me to soothe them. This would bring out my soft, nurturing side—something I needed. The puppy I'd get would be calm and help soothe me too. Actually, I thought more about *being* soothed than soothing. After all, dogs were supposed to bring unconditional love, no judgment, no argument. I realize now that I wanted a dog for the wrong reasons, with mistaken expectations.

This puppy did indeed meet my gaze, but it was often to say, *I have a better idea* or *Are you sure about that?* His stare was steady, unblinking. Fifteen years later I would seek that stare, even in spirit. Fifteen years later I would know the strength of the connection I had with this dog in physical reality, and even in the realm of the invisible. But right now I was anchored in that "real" material world, governed by my five senses. A dog was a dog, and I was a human who knew little about the being who had entered my life. And yet—there was something about him that I could feel even then, although I could not fathom it.

It was a point in my life that called for honesty. I could not evade looking at my situation: a long-standing relationship with a man had ended badly. He said I was his soul mate, and now he was marrying someone else. Whom could I trust? I had no prospect by this time of having children. My father died young when I was in college. My mother, nearing ninety, was in a nursing home, becoming more mentally distant every day. When I looked at the world I saw other people in relationships, with someone. I walked alone. I didn't want to walk alone anymore.

There had been a trigger for this self-confrontation. A few months before, I was jolted into the realization that there should be more to my life than work. I was in a serious car accident during a film shoot in Nevada. The SUV rolled over three times on a dirt road. It was like being tumbled in a wave, but the wave was all metal—sharp parts and crashing. I had a seat belt on and I luckily survived with only a concussion. But any assumptions that I had plenty of time to change my life had literally been knocked out of me. Afterward, I wanted to feel connected to something.

I'd been a lonely child—an only child. I had no siblings. People remarked that I didn't talk very much in social company. I felt somehow apart. My father was often absent, traveling for work. My mother was overprotective. She'd lost a daughter in still birth before she had me. Throughout my early childhood we were very comfortable financially. In that sense I was secure. I also felt great pressure, however, to live up to a family that was filled with very accomplished and, in some cases, famous people. It was clear that there were high expectations for me.

I remember that I felt a need—not defined or even conscious at the time—to hold myself separate, to try to set my own course. But that meant a kind of self-isolation. I had good friends, but as I recall I never shared my deepest fears and most private thoughts with them. In fact, my most intimate connections with living beings were with animals. They were my salvation. We had a Siamese cat when I was growing up. When I felt I couldn't talk to anyone else, or when I went to bed at night—sometimes alone in the house with a babysitter when my parents were out—it was Maki the cat who was my confidant and comforter. He lay on the bed. I talked to him and put my hand on him.

I also remembered the joy I'd felt with animals as a child. I felt it first with the family cats, and then later with other people's dogs. I also felt it riding my horse. I wanted to feel that joy again, now in the present moment, when all around me was repetition and routine. With animals, I felt centered; I felt like myself—my true self.

That's when I realized I wanted to get a dog. I had the idea that they shared one's life. They went out with you and met people. They connected you with the world. So I started obsessively researching breeders. I'd settled on standard poodles because I'd known a family friend's poodles as a child.

But the idea of getting a dog was completely impractical. I was middle-aged. While my personal life may have looked like a failure, my professional life was a resounding success. I was at the height of my career as an award-winning television documentary and news producer. I traveled constantly across the country and around the world. When friends and colleagues heard I was thinking of getting a dog they raised their eyebrows at me and told me, "Don't do it." They begged me to understand that a dog required time and commitment, neither of which I had at the moment. Most of my friends thought I was crazy. Actually, so did I.

No doubt people also thought that my personality—at least what had become the exterior of my personality—was not exactly a custom fit with dog ownership. I suspect people were more worried about the dog than about me. I had a reputation for toughness in my professional life and coldness personally. At work, I was demanding of myself and of the people who worked with me. I lacked patience. I lacked tact. I brooked no foolishness. I didn't deal with people very well. I didn't communicate well. So what in the world made me think I could communicate with a *dog*?

There's no doubt about it. The dog decision made no sense at all, but still, I was bound and determined. Perhaps it was my destiny that pushed me into the choice in order to transform my life. Or maybe it was my intuitive voice—with which I had never connected prior to Brio's existence—that whispered, *Do it.*

I launched into the dog purchase as I would have into a television story, gathering information, weighing options. Deep down, I was terrified. When I sat alone in my small apartment at night I could not imagine having a puppy running around in there. How could I think? How could I work? I had never made a commitment to another living being apart from my mother for whose care I was now responsible. But a dog? I would be responsible 24/7. The puppy would be totally dependent on me even if I hired help. I couldn't even imagine the stress of feeling the presence of the puppy in my apartment constantly, leaving paw prints on the floor and drool marks on the couch. How could I go out? How could I have a social life? I did indeed ask myself those questions. But then I'd try to shut down that voice in my head and press on with the puppy search.

It was finally some sense of fate, I suppose, that moved me a step ahead. I'd seen a female poodle strutting down the road on Martha's Vineyard, where I go, when possible, to breathe the sea air and hear the ocean. Something about that dog's attitude appealed to me. She looked like she enjoyed her world. So I asked for her breeder's name and called down to Virginia that day. It turned out the breeder had a new litter born on the birthday of a dear friend of mine. It seemed like the stars were aligned—even though at the time I didn't believe in that sort of thing.

I had a plan. I would get a female poodle. Everyone said they were easier to have in the city. A male could mark in the house and run away after a girl in the park. Females were smaller, lighter, easier to handle. The first visit to the breeder cemented the plan.

So—I find myself on the floor of a roomy Virginia farmhouse, surrounded by a litter of small, very loud and squirming, scrambling puppies. Just off the plane from New York, I'm following the breeder's suggestion to get down on their level and see which one of these tiny creatures I'm drawn to. They're only a month old, not even looking like fully formed puppies. "Are you sure it's not too early to tell about their personalities?" I ask the breeder, Lynn.

"Not at all," she says, pointing out how some puppies hang back shyly while some push their way to the mother, bullying their siblings. The mayhem on the floor feels like the other side of the looking glass, a place that's the reverse image of my normally controlled, orderly, and outwardly unsentimental approach to life. One puppy in particular is doing everything possible to get me to notice him, but I am playing no favorites, trying to make a reasoned decision about which—if any—of the littermates will fit into my world.

The feisty puppy is putting on a spectacular exhibition, trotting up and down, up and down. He runs and waves his paw at me, runs off again, and then comes back waving. *True,* I say to myself, *he is charismatic.* There's something compelling about his energy and exuberance. But I feel overwhelmed. There's a very loud voice in my head asking: *What am I doing? A dog like this is not meant for me. I'm not exactly sure that any dog is meant for me.* I am surprised at the near terror and inde-cision I am feeling. I'm not used to feeling hesitant. I'm a professional woman, accustomed to pressure, comfortable making big decisions. But suddenly, confronted with these puppies, I'm filled with doubt and fear. All the reasons that made me think I wanted a dog in the first place seem ridiculous to me now.

"Apparently he's picked you instead of vice versa," the breeder says of the feisty puppy. "He's the pick of the litter, though," she cautions. "My co-breeder may end up taking him."

Frankly I'm relieved, though I don't tell her that. My plan is to get a female anyway.

"Oh that's okay," I say, pushing the boy puppy off my lap. "He's much too much for me. What about that quiet little girl over there in the corner?"

Lynn looks a bit disappointed in me and gently remarks that often boy poodles are "sweeter" than the girls, who she says can be "manip-ulative." But she accepts my deposit on the beautiful girl puppy who catches my fancy. I'm to come back in a few weeks when the puppies are old enough to go to their new homes.

I thought that would probably be the last I saw of the exuberant boy. I'd made my plans for the girl. But there were apparently other designs in motion. I didn't realize it at the time, but I was already in the hands of something larger than myself.

A few weeks later, I got a call from the breeder. The exuberant black boy puppy had indeed been the pick of the litter. The co-breeder had wanted him, but one of his testicles had not "fallen," making him unsuitable for breeding. So the co-breeder decided to take the charming black female instead. Only one puppy was left. Yes, of course. It was the feisty black puppy who had picked me from the beginning! Here was my first lesson among many that I would learn from my dog about the power of letting go and surrendering to the flow of the universe.

So back I went to the breeder, and there I was, face-to-face with the black puppy. He stared me right in the eyes—there was an enchanting familiarity in his gaze, almost as if I had looked into his eyes on many past occasions. His expression seemed to say, *It's up to you. What are you going to do?* He wasn't pleading. He certainly didn't seem sorry for himself, being the last puppy left. He just looked, acknowledging me, and waited. Somehow in that moment, I found myself unable to say no to him. It would not be the last time.

So I made the decision to take him as soon as I got back from a trip overseas. The day came. As I took him in my arms for the first time, it felt like a dream. I couldn't tell if it was a good dream or a nightmare though, because I just didn't feel like myself. I was going through the motions but in a trancelike state. It seemed I was watching someone else, some stranger getting his or her first dog. Through this daze, I heard the breeder's friend—who'd brought the puppy to meet me at National Airport in Washington—say with tears in her eyes: "Give him a good life. He's special." Finally back on terra firma in New York City, I hailed a cab and careened through the traffic toward home. It was a sweltering September day with inadequate air conditioning in the taxi. The open windows blew gusts of hot air. I dripped with sweat and stress.

"We'll be alright, everything is fine, we're going to have a great life together," I said to the puppy, who was peering at me through the narrow openings of his travel crate. He lay with his front paws spread in front him; his puppy eyes, visible under a full head of black curls, gazing not quite at me but at something out in space perhaps. He clearly had his own thoughts, and I wondered if he knew he was riding home with a very anxious human who believed she had stepped beyond the bounds of reason. He did not seem anxious himself, merely detached—reserving judgment about his situation.

At last we arrived at my apartment in a New York City high-rise. I let the puppy out of his crate and put him into the pen I had created in the kitchen. It was lined with paper in anticipation of his arrival. I tried to imagine how this little dog must have felt on his flight from Virginia, locked in a cage, thrust among bags and boxes, ears hammered by noise, struggling to use his sense of smell to decipher the chaos around him. I imagined him paralyzed with fear, traumatized for life. And now this strange small space, penned in a tiny kitchen with newspapers all over the floor—so far from the glorious Virginia farm where he'd been born. I offered him water and waited for him to relieve himself in the place I'd provided. I waited. And nothing happened. Neither of us knew what to do next. I sat down on the floor. He collapsed in my lap, and I did what all panicked first-time parents do—I called in a professional.

"Lynn, we're home," I said to the breeder, but there definitely was no relief in my voice.

"How is he?" Lynn asked in her gentle southern voice.

"He's fallen asleep in my lap," I told her with a tone of utter exhaustion and helplessness.

"That's good, it's a sign he's started to bond with you," Lynn reassured me, and although my legs were going numb from his weight, and I wanted nothing more in that moment than to have a shower and then go out for dinner with a friend, I felt encouraged. Bonding was something I had expected from this new endeavor, and here this puppy was already fulfilling expectations.

Then suddenly my new possession—as I thought of him—got up from my lap, walked in the opposite direction of the newspaper, and let loose everything that he had been holding in for hours on the plane, all over my kitchen floor. I stood there paralyzed, unsure what to do beyond grabbing the newspapers and soaking everything up. My fight-or-flight response took over and I picked up the phone and dialed the breeder.

"Lynn?" I croaked into the phone that I held with one hand as I struggled with the mess.

"Yes, how's it going?" Lynn asked, not revealing a hint of impatience or the exasperation she surely must have been feeling at that moment.

"I'm really not sure I can do this. You said I could bring him back, right? I just don't think I can manage this. It's too much," I said, and in that moment, I felt exasperated with myself.

Lynn was indeed a professional. She expressed no surprise or objection. Perhaps she'd heard this before and knew that after the first twenty-four hours there would be no way that puppy was coming back. He was just too irresistible. Or perhaps she knew better than me that we were actually a perfect match.

"Certainly," Lynn said placidly, "you can bring him back. But why don't you give it a week or so? See how things go. Give you both a chance to get to know each other."

"Alright," I said and looked at the puppy, who looked right back at me, not at all embarrassed about the havoc he had just wreaked in my fastidiously arranged kitchen. And that's when I decided *yes*—it was time for this puppy to learn his name. After all, how were we going to communicate with each other unless I named him?

"Your name is Brio," I told him, and loved the way it sounded coming out of my mouth. "Do you like your name, Brio? Brio?" Brio seemed unimpressed and began to doze off again in my lap. "It's a musical term in Italian. It means 'enthusiasm, vigor, vivacity, verve.' That's you, Brio." Maybe it was the tone of my voice, but Brio looked at me with what seemed like acknowledgment. Apparently I had chosen a name he approved of.

The name had come to me weeks before, perhaps even before I had made the final decision to take him. There were many classical musicians in my family, and it seemed to make sense to gift my dog with a name that was musical. I may not have realized when I chose the name exactly how suitable it would be.

Yet at some level it spoke to a spirit, an energy that I sought myself. *I* wanted to have brio. From the start, I was asking this dog to change me. What a huge demand. How little I understood what I was really asking.

2

Why Doesn't My Puppy Love Me?

IT DIDN'T TAKE LONG FOR BRIO TO EMBODY HIS NAME. My idea that the puppy would be happily confined to the kitchen area where he would sleep, eat, and go to the bathroom soon collapsed, as did the gate I'd erected between kitchen and living room.

"Brio, no! You can't go in there!" I'd shout fruitlessly as he tore through the living room into the bedroom and then into the bathroom.

"No, no . . . don't pee *there*!" I squeaked, catching him mid-squat. I carried him back onto the newspapers in the kitchen, where he cut loose once again. *Well, at least we made it to the paper,* his eyes seemed to say to me. That was progress.

As the week went along, I must confess I felt invaded. My life had been completely taken over. I had imagined that since a dog would belong to me I would feel that I belonged. I would feel attached and connected to life. Instead my barriers were up. I felt I was losing my sense of self, of who I was. I didn't know what to do with this very active, very alive being who clearly had his own mind and personality and who was thoroughly taking over my life.

Brio was becoming the center of my existence in terms of physical demands on my time. I would go to work and feel huge relief at being

11

in a familiar world for a few hours where there wasn't a black streak rushing past me on his way to breaking another household rule. But I also felt terrible leaving the puppy at home in the crate while he was being paper-trained. In the city, he wasn't supposed to go outside until he'd had all his shots; he could catch something from other dogs on the street. I had someone coming in during the day to put him on the newspaper occasionally, but I'd think about him all day long and worry about his feelings. He was a prisoner in that tiny apartment. Perhaps, I realized, I should have thought more about what this would be like for him. When I came home, emotionally I felt a great distance between us. We seemed to be strangers to each other. Shouldn't this be easier?

Still, every night I would put him in a crate beside my bed. I'd reach down to touch him through the crate's openings. I had tried leaving him in the crate out near the kitchen, but he cried—as he cried every time I left the house.

During those first days and nights together, exhaustion was foremost in my mind and heart. The newspaper bathroom idea soon bit the dust. I couldn't stand it. So out on the street we went every few hours—all through the night. I would avoid other dogs, hiding in corners. Inside, when Brio wasn't crated, I sat on the kitchen floor and worked there so as to defend against the storming of the dog gate. I was in survival mode and nearly falling asleep at my desk. So I decided it was time to call in help and get Brio trained so I could restore sanity and control in my home.

As usual, I went at the project of finding a trainer for Brio as if I were making a documentary and researched every trainer in a four-state radius. I settled on a very famous trainer, Bash Dibra. Bash came to the house and found Brio squeezed into his crate, which was filled with sheepskin to the point that he couldn't turn around. Bash is renowned for his charismatic effect on dogs. Brio was no exception; once liberated from the stuffed crate, he ran for Bash as if to a savior. I was humiliated. Clearly, the puppy had bonded more with Bash in a few seconds than he had with me in days. There it was. My puppy didn't like me, I concluded sadly.

And honestly, I couldn't blame him. He'd been stuffed into a crate unable to easily move or turn around for days. I felt like an idiot. Had I ruined any chance of connection between us forever? Would he ever trust me to take proper care of him again? But Bash reassured me as well as Brio, and we started our work together. The first time Brio "officially" went out on the street (after having had his shots), he trotted boldly forward, tail straight up, looking like he owned the world.

"He won't have any problem in the city; he has total confidence that he can handle anything," Bash said, and I could see he was impressed with Brio. But to me, it just seemed to reinforce the idea that this puppy didn't need me. He was his own person.

Brio had a stubborn streak. The flip side of his confidence was his ability to tune out any instructions that conflicted with his own desires. Bash, however, seemed to have a way to get through to him with some special charismatic power. "Come," Bash would call, and most of the time the puppy who normally couldn't wait to run off now couldn't wait to run to Bash.

"How did you do that?" I would ask.

"Brio has a special spirit," Bash said. "He's got a special stallion kind of spirit. He doesn't want to be led, but he also respects others. I love that quality in him so I say, 'Oh Brio, you and I have an understanding.'"

As the days went by, I found I was becoming increasingly jealous of the bond that Bash and Brio were building. Clearly, he had no problem understanding and communicating with Brio. In the presence of their bond, I felt I didn't stand a chance.

Because I was desperate to get Brio in some kind of working order, I swallowed my jealousy and I called in Bash again. I had to at least get Brio to come when I called. Otherwise there was no way he could be off the leash in New York City's Central Park—the only backyard we had. This time, Bash arrived with a very long lead line, and off to the park we went. When Brio bolted off toward the tree line of a large field, he abruptly reached the end of the rope. This was alarming. Even Bash was shaken. "That was a bad bolt," he remarked. *That's an understatement,*

I thought, for in witnessing the debacle I had feared that Brio might be strangled. Furthermore, the next day he continued to run and run when I tried letting him off the leash. No doubt he knew I didn't have the stomach for the long-line treatment. (Hence, the incident when he ran off and I fell into the pond!)

When I walked Brio by myself the training lessons seemed to fade into distant memory. I forgot how to properly give the commands, and I tended to repeat "heel, heel, heel" with futile jerks on the leash. Most of the time I gave up too soon, and Brio would confidently take over the lead from me, charging down the street with me in tow. People would ask as we raced passed: "Hey, who's walking whom there?" I began to ask myself the same thing, as I realized that Brio was beginning to teach me far more than I was teaching him.

So it went. My pre-puppy expectation that my dog would be completely dependent on me, accompanied by obedience and devotion, disappeared day by revelatory day. Tears sometimes came with the growing conviction that the relationship was not going in the proper direction. That was the issue. The unconditional love promised to new dog owners seemed inextricably linked to the quality of dependence. The dog needs the owner; the owner must be in control. But Brio seemed to need neither my acceptance nor my approval. Clearly, I was doing something very wrong. Brio and I must not be a good match.

Here I was in yet another failed relationship. I couldn't make it work—not even with a dog! That's where I was in the crazy chatter of my thoughts.

The trainers, Bash and a few others I called on from time to time, did eventually provide a language to communicate with Brio on some basic level. Yet there remained this odd distance between us—in my mind. There was a sense that he lived in his own world, one that I just didn't know how to enter. Brio was an alien creature to me. I didn't speak "dog." And that's how I still saw him at this point—as a dog, a dog I wanted to master and a dog from whom I expected unconditional love.

I was feeling worse and worse about myself. I felt sorry for Brio being stuck with a person who clearly was not suited to warm, loving, nurturing relationships. I know! I know! I had expected a lot from this puppy. I'd wanted a lot more than probably was fair to ask. Maybe he was the wrong dog, but inside I felt I was the wrong *person*. I'd tried to get a dog to change me, and it seemed an impossible idea.

I'd expected to learn the language of dog in the sense of "sit," "stay," "down." I planned to work with trainers and achieve some degree of communication that would make life manageable. Of course what I imagined was really using my language to train the puppy to do what I wanted. This, for me, felt "safe." The goal was to be in charge, after all—just as I was at work. My parents loved animals, but I never got any idea from them that our household animals were more than pets— I held onto the notion that they were creatures that were beloved but whose understanding was clearly subordinate to that of humans. Day by day, Brio was challenging that assumption.

As time passed, I noticed that Brio was capable of discernment and even humor. He showed a sense of wit and clear intent. He rarely chewed the furniture or shoes—normal puppy targets. Instead, he purposefully went for my work papers, the very things that constantly took my attention away from him. Files left on the desk during even a brief absence would be shredded upon my return. He showed no sign of guilt, perhaps just the quiver of a sly smile that broadened when I deserted the papers to play, throwing his ball in the hallway outside the tiny apartment. He made the best of the cramped quarters and lack of a yard. Nothing fazed him. I couldn't help but sometimes wonder what my life would be like if I too let nothing bother me.

Despite myself, underneath all the anxiety and doubts, I was coming to adore him. He was a puppy playmate who could chase balls and catch Frisbees and roll in the grass, legs beating the air. He breathed life into the city and brought the world of childhood fun alive. He went with me to the nursing home to visit my mother and turned back the sadness as he chased his ball and climbed into her lap. He loved to shop because he got so much attention and admiration. He would park himself in the middle of a store—sometimes lying on a cool floor in the summer—and wait for people to gather around him. And he loved music—especially Bach. When I would play Bach on the stereo or on my cello, he would roll over on the couch and put all four feet in the air.

All of this was a new and revelatory experience for me! I found it was easy to meet and talk to people with him at my side—so much easier than when I was alone. I had a support system to help walk him or board him when I was busy with work. I now welcomed our trips around the neighborhood together. He was certainly "walking me"—teaching me despite myself. He also led me in directions I'd never anticipated. I'd grown up with cats and loved them. But my feeling for cats was nothing compared to the obsession that Brio came to develop for them.

It started when he actually "rescued" a little black cat who had escaped out of a ground floor window and was sitting on the windowsill. Brio would not move from the cat until I banged on the window, drawing the attention of the man who lived there, who brought the cat safely back inside. From then on, Brio looked for cats. He went back to that same window all the time looking for the black cat. Often we saw him. And Brio pulled me into pet shops, not interested in the puppies, but making a beeline for the kittens. To make a long story short, this obsession eventually resulted in the acquisition of Brio's own kitten. Brio's wish—my command!

I realized that I loved looking at him. I loved his face cascading with black curls. He had a broad forehead, even as a puppy, with this full head of hair framing it and long, full ears. He didn't always seem rooted in the world around him, but aloft in some other realm. I imagined he was contemplating higher truths. Still, even by now he remained in many ways a stranger to me. I acknowledged that this was the most uncomfortable thing about Brio's presence: I couldn't figure him out.

That unsettling sense of distance with a living being who shared my space and life was what ultimately led me to venture beyond the world of reason, logic, and known reality into an alternate universe, one that called for belief in the invisible, in intuition, in matters of spirit. It's possible I had been seeking to take this route for a long time, but Brio's sometimes awkward presence fueled my courage to finally take the first step down the long winding road of faith in matters unseen. I know it was also my journalistic nature and insatiable need to get to the "bottom of things" that made me turn my attention to explanations beyond the rational, material world.

I had come to find out after much research that there were people who claimed to be able to read dogs' minds, to somehow translate what they are thinking into human language. I was curious though largely disbelieving. Nothing in my heritage, education, or beliefs would have predicted the journey on which I was about to embark. I was not religious, not even spiritual—whatever *that* term meant!

I belonged to a family of artists and intellectuals. My father, from a long line of Jewish musicians, had been a pianist and a scientist. He had claimed to be an atheist, or at least an agnostic, and Judaism and religion were never even mentioned in a family that identified itself not with faith but with the "our crowd" elite. My mother had a Protestant background but never attended church. I was taught above all to have a critical mind, to question belief systems, and to shun anything smacking of a cult at all costs. I can hear the scornful laughter now, at the mention of psychics or the paranormal. It replayed many times in my head during the strange investigations I undertook. Yet my wish to create a deeper relationship with my dog drove me into new territory— foreign to me and to my background.

I had such an inexplicable attraction to Brio and his lingering mystery that I needed to know what was really going on in his head in a way that even dog trainers couldn't explain to my satisfaction.

I wanted to feel a sense of intimacy. And perhaps I longed to feel it with other human beings as well. I would work my way up to that. For now I would start here, and prove to myself that a meaningful connection with my dog was possible.

So I took a deep breath and picked up the phone.

The first animal communicator I contacted was based in California.

Like many animal psychics, she professed to be able to do her work by phone without even meeting the animal in question. As impossible as this sounded, I decided to try it, as an experiment. *Just an experiment,* I told myself.

So I called Samantha Khury, a well-known animal communicator at the time. I had seen her picture in an article—she was an attractive and friendly looking blonde woman. On the phone, she asked in a calm voice how she could help me.

"I have a standard poodle puppy who's my first dog," I told her. "I'd like to know more about what's going on in his mind because I feel I can't communicate with him as well as I'd like." I didn't want to tell her much about Brio. I also didn't tell her anything about myself except that I lived in New York City, which she could figure out from the area code anyway. I wanted to reduce the odds that she could guess answers or deduce things about Brio from information she gleaned from me in advance (typical of me). I stood firm.

She asked for his name, appearance, and age and then proceeded to describe my apartment as if seen through Brio's eyes. As I sat at my small desk, staring out from the twenty-seventh-floor window of my apartment, I heard: "He really likes the big wide window. He says it lets in a lot of light. He likes that." I was startled at the accuracy of her insights. I did have that big wide window that looked over an open view eastward, letting in the morning sun. At night the buildings nearby would reflect the sunset through the window too.

"He says he's figured out how to run around the apartment around all the things," Samantha continued on. Again, I felt the thrill of authenticity. I did have a small apartment, with quite a bit of furniture.

"And do you live on a wide street?" she asked. "Because he says he likes it better when you walk on a smaller street." Right again.

My interest was whetted. I by no means considered this proof that Samantha could read Brio's mind. Even if she was psychic, perhaps she was reading *my* mind, not the dog's. Still, something tugged at me. What she said felt like what Brio would "say." And after all I had no preference for the street on which we walked. But maybe he did.

I started out seeking evidence and confirmation, wanting to know certain things for sure. I remained unconvinced, though intrigued. In the end, I wanted to know what Brio thought about his life, about me. I suppose I wanted to know that he loved me even though at the time I suspected that maybe he wasn't too sure about me at all. I had begun to think that this connection and communication I was searching for would never be possible between Brio and me.

Still, Samantha Khury had opened the first door of possibility. I realized though that if I acknowledged that Brio had thoughts and feelings like humans beings do, then the whole concept of dogs—all animals for that matter—as inferior beings under human control needed to be reconsidered.

I had never really contemplated the conflict between the need for authority over animals and the need for a relationship with them, which is, of course, as old as human history. Cultures worldwide have fables in which human traits are attributed to animals both real and imagined. Take the example of the unicorn, a creature first mentioned in ancient Greece. It achieved great stature in the Middle Ages and during the Renaissance as a symbol of purity and grace, with special powers to heal. In Native American culture, it's believed that human beings have animal "totems," or guides, that help us through life. The unshakable connection between human and animal then takes on a spiritual dimension.

No such lofty thoughts occurred to me in the early months of my life with Brio, however. I had a puppy en route to being a teenager, not a unicorn. But now I just knew that there was something behind those dark eyes beyond what I had expected. I was in very foreign territory with a living creature I didn't know how to decipher. There was the inkling of the idea that perhaps this curlicued black dervish could teach me something if I could hear what he had to say as a being in his own right, not as one I hoped to shape and control.

I found myself trying to please him, even comfort him, although he was so independent and confident. It was really for me; I wanted him to need me, to show me that we had a connection. On our first long-distance car trip from the city en route to a vacation in the country, he started to become car sick, riding on the backseat. I brought him up front and he climbed into my lap, resting his head on the bottom of the steering wheel. It was a bit awkward to steer, but I managed. Brio was fine right there for the rest of the journey. The moment is strong in my memory. He'd felt that he wouldn't be queasy and insecure in my lap. In that moment, he'd found what he needed with me. Yet I know he'd met a greater need in me. We had come together; we'd connected. Of course he took it all in stride. He just accepted that he'd found a solution that let him relax. No worries, he seemed to be saying. All is well.

I kept trying for more of that connection. There was something in Brio's energy that I recognized as something I wanted for myself, something I craved to be able to express myself despite the reserved, controlling, and self-preserved appearance I presented to the world. There was a familiarity in Brio's way of being, and a longing within me to be as happy and careless as he seemed to be. Brio loved to run. Flat-out down the beach, into the fog, he was gone with the wind, nose to the salt air, flying through the ocean spray. At that moment, he was simply himself. Pure freedom. Instinctively I felt, even then, that it was more than that. I saw a being taking life on his own terms.

As he reached a year old, he had become a magnificent dog, reveling in his power and speed. It was clear he knew how handsome he was. He held his head high above his solid neck and broad shoulders. "I am me," he was saying. "Enjoy me as I enjoy myself." While I constantly struggled to change others, my circumstances, and myself, Brio was perfectly fine being exactly who and what he was. Most ironically, he had perfect control over life because he didn't try to take control over life; he existed in acceptance and harmony with what was around him.

I wanted Brio's energy, his confidence, his freedom, his joy. I wanted to feel it. I had embarked on a journey to know Brio—a journey in fact to know myself. It would take me places I'd never dreamed of going.

3
Wake-Up Calls

WE'RE IN THE FLOWER SHOP AGAIN, enveloped in fragrance. Roses, lilies, freesia—a heady nectar. I had not planned on going in. Brio, as he always did when we passed the store, had pulled me in, not for a biscuit or to greet the owner but simply to smell. He sat absorbing it all. And I stood forced to take it in with him, to appreciate it with him, something no one had ever taught me to do before. It was my first lesson in patience.

For all his exuberance, there was a profound stillness in Brio. At the beach he would stare out to sea, into the horizon. In the city, he sought out flower shops. In these moments, he was in his own world. Even sitting, senses at work as he parsed his surroundings, there was something compelling about him. He was so still, so focused—but on what, I still didn't know.

There was majesty about him—a magnetism. And it wasn't just personality. He seemed to have a palpable energy, an aura that I came to think of as "presence." With him, I felt more awake, more alive, more centered. I was supposed to be walking him. Yet he'd pull me into a moment amid the flowers. I had to wonder: who was really at the end of the leash? Did it even matter? No one in my life had ever led me to stop and literally smell the roses. Brio did.

Our life together in New York City gradually settled into a routine. There were the early morning walks to Central Park, where Brio could run off the leash at that time of day. He would still sometimes literally "run off"! But I was growing to trust that eventually he would come back. Then I moved to a new apartment, which meant a new neighborhood. But Brio adapted very quickly—both indoors and out. The night after I'd moved, with the apartment full of boxes, I looked around and found him lying on the couch, where he'd never been allowed to be in the old place. I didn't have the heart to move him—as he no doubt knew. So from then on the couch was his.

I certainly had no experience with the dog-human connection when I hesitantly came to this relationship. I'd naively thought that the only way dogs and people could talk to each other was through programmed human words or physical gestures—commands. Now I was beginning to think in a very different way about Brio, about who he was, about his capacity to feel and his level of intelligence. So I also had to think differently about how to communicate with him.

Dog people who have experience and insight know well that dogs read us like a book. Considerable research has been done looking at why dogs, uniquely among domesticated animals, seem to be so attuned to humans and able to pick up our body language, our feelings, and even our thoughts so accurately. There's evidence that dogs are more able to understand the world from a human perspective than had been previously recognized.

In a recent study, when the lights were turned off so the humans in the room couldn't see them, dogs were four times more likely to steal food they had been forbidden (than when the lights were on). Dr. Juliane Kaminski, who performed this study at the University of Portsmouth in the United Kingdom, says, "It's unlikely that the dogs simply forgot that the human was in the room" when there was no light. It seemed, Kaminski contends, that the dogs actually could tell when the human was likely to see them and adapted their behavior accordingly. "The current finding," the study reports, "raises the possibility that dogs take into account the human's visual access to the food while making their decision to steal it."[1]

Another recent study shows that dogs can decipher the emotion behind vocal communication in the same way that humans can. Brain scans conducted by the Comparative Ethology Research Group in Hungary found that dog and human brains both lit up in the voice areas of the brain—which are in similar locations in both species—when whining, crying, happy barks, and laughing were heard. Moreover, in both species the auditory cortex showed more activation when a happy sound was heard versus a sad one. The researchers believe the study presents evidence that dogs and humans share an emotional "language."[2] We have, after all, evolved alongside each other for the past one hundred thousand years.

Neuroscientist Gregory Berns of Emory University conducted brain scans of dogs that also strongly indicated that they have emotional responses similar to humans. The same brain area, called the caudate, which is associated with enjoyment in people, is activated in the dog brain in response to a hand signal indicating food.[3]

I always sensed, when I sat on the beach with Brio, staring out at the ocean, that we were feeling the same wonder and peace and awe in the space we shared. When something pleased him, he would get a little smile on his face. He often had that smile as he looked to the sea.

Yet another study indicates that dogs not only understand the emotions behind our words but that they also can comprehend the meanings of words no matter what the accompanying inflection or emotion. A graduate psychology student at the University of Sussex in England did an experiment in which she played a recorded command to 250 dogs with and without inflections in the speaker's voice. She then recorded which way the dogs turned their heads and found a clear pattern of difference, depending on whether they heard meaningful words or just emotional cues. The results indicate that the dog's brain—like the human brain—is separating speech into two parts: the emotional cues and the meaning of words.[4]

Early in the twentieth century, animal cognition research was discredited by the case of a horse in Germany, Clever Hans. It was claimed that he could understand human words and do mathematical calculations. Then it was shown that he was actually responding to body language cues from his human handler. Still, pretty clever![5]

Today's current science has marked a sea change in how we think of the nature and abilities of nonhuman animals. I had increasingly come to recognize Brio as an autonomous and sentient being. When one sees one's own dog in this way, one cannot help but become more aware of how we treat all our fellow beings.

Recent research has led some scientists to argue for the legal rights of animals. Three prominent neuroscientists recently issued a declaration saying that "nonhuman animals have the neuroanatomical, neurochemical, and neurophysiological substrates of conscious states along with the capacity to exhibit intentional behaviors."[6]

Here we have scientists delving into the mysterious realm of consciousness.

Science has yet to decipher the nature of human consciousness, much less that of other species. Yet the exploration itself shows that some scientists are driven by curiosity about what's going on inside animals' minds and who they really are.

I could see that Brio made decisions about what to do in certain situations and knew to make other choices in different circumstances. He was clearly able to choose his moments to do exactly what he wanted, completely ignoring what was in *my* mind about his behavior. Once when I was hosting a cocktail party in the country, he seized a moment when I was distracted to somehow get out of the house and run very fast and very far down the road, after a deer. It took a good ten minutes of chasing him in my heeled sandals down the dirt path, screaming in panic, before he deigned to hear me and turn around.

I was becoming aware of Brio as not "just a dog" but as a conscious being. He constantly exhibited a creative and original mind. Once when he was still quite young, I took him with me to dinner at the home of some friends. He disappeared for a bit. After calling him for several minutes with no results, we searched the house. We found him in a back bedroom sitting on a nightstand next to a tall lamp. The perch gave him an excellent view out the window.

I came to realize that I would never be able to make Brio "obey" and "sit" the way I wanted, and I was grateful for it. I was starting to see that he was his own master and a unique being.

Other people seemed to sense some special quality in Brio. My close friends, Bob and Arline Prince, knew poodles well. They'd owned several over the years and in fact helped inspire my affection for the breed as well as Brio's name. Bob Prince was a composer, and their dog, Forte, had also been named after a musical term.

One night at dinner we were talking about our respective dogs' personalities. "Forte is a genius, the smartest dog we ever had," Bob remarked with pride and a touch of dog-person competitiveness. "Look at what he does when I sing 'Oh Danny Boy' to him—but as 'Oh Downy Boy!'" Sure enough, after a couple of phrases Forte slid his front paws forward into a "down."

"He won't do that if you just say 'down'?" I asked.

"Only when I sing," Bob replied with a smile. He was not a fan of traditional dog training, but it was clear he was really enjoying this exhibition of canine comprehension techniques. I was impressed and a little competitive myself.

"Brio's smart too, don't you think?" I asked, fishing for confirmation of my growing conviction that Brio was special.

Bob was not a man to get into deep conversation about matters of spirit and soul. He held his inner feelings and insights about life to himself. So what he said next surprised and touched me. He looked intently at me, as though he wanted me to really hear what he was saying. "He's not just smart," he said evenly. "You can look into his eyes and see the pyramids." I felt chills along my arms. Bob had seen what I saw in Brio each day—that eternal presence, a kind of wisdom that was deep and ancient.

A year or so after the conversation with Bob, I decided to visit an ayurvedic doctor to ask about nutrition and diet for myself. A friend had recommended this healer and I was curious. I decided to take Brio with me because I didn't have a dog walker that day. We waited in the office with lots of people for our turn to be called in. Brio sat like a statue. He tended to rise to occasions like this and restrain his exuberant tendencies. Finally the healer, Pankaj Naram, a sweet Indian man in a long jacket, beckoned us into his room.

"Oh, he's an old soul," were Dr. Naram's first words, looking intently at Brio.

"What do you mean?" I asked, both excited that he had picked up on Brio's special quality and a bit nervous about what would come next. Who was Brio exactly? Was I living with a being who really had come from some other dimension and who had knowledge completely foreign to me? Part of me feared learning that Brio was actually some kind of old master in dog's clothing—not even my equal but a being whose essence I could never fathom and certainly never control. With Dr. Naram's next words, I really felt stunned.

"He's been here on Earth many times," said the healer, peering into Brio's eyes as if he was making out a story there. "He won't be coming back as a dog in the next life, we know that."

"He's coming back? What do you mean *coming back*?" I asked. Brio was young. I certainly wasn't thinking of the end of his life, much less a *return* to life. But in the back of my mind I had some fear that if he came back it might not be to me. I might not recognize or see him again.

"You'll be surprised," the healer said to me cryptically, and then turned his attention to my questions about my diet. Nonetheless, during most of the visit, he remained in silent but substantive conversation with Brio.

Sometimes I got surprising reports from people who said Brio had somehow changed their lives. A housekeeper confided that she told Brio her secrets when I wasn't around. There was something about him, she said, that made her know he understood—understood and did not judge. Then Jim Moran, a former computer technology expert turned dog walker, let me know that Brio played a key role in his decision to make that major career change. Jim had first turned to dog walking as temporary work when he'd been laid off from a corporate tech job and was still looking for work in that field. One day he was out walking Brio in a snowstorm. "He loved the snow and the wind. I was having a great time with him," Jim remembers. "It was idyllic." And then his cell phone rang. It was a headhunter offering him a big job with Hewlett-Packard. The headhunter talked about all the money that came with the job. Meanwhile, Jim says, "Brio is playing in the snow and I'm having a ball watching him." Jim thought about the pressure and harassment from complaining clients that would also come with the job. In that moment, watching Brio, Jim decided to turn down the work and to "reinvent myself as a dog walker and trainer." The moment with Brio gave him clarity. "That was fifteen years ago," he says, "and I haven't regretted that decision once since then."

These acknowledgments from other people validated what I by now felt myself. I felt safe with Brio. I felt able to stay in the moment, secure in the moment, even in very difficult situations. The night my mother died in a nursing home, Brio went with me to sit with her body. He sat perfectly still by my side, looking at her. He allowed me to look at her and to accept the reality of that moment, to feel it and to live with it.

Others clearly felt Brio's presence, his consciousness, even if they didn't call it by those specific names or know exactly what it was that they sensed. The comments moved me down the road into a mysterious territory of the unexplainable and the invisible. There would soon be more wake-up calls to come.

Fueled by my growing belief in the consciousness of animals, I thought of ways I could introduce my newfound curiosity into my work. *How can I do some more research about animal communication?* I wondered. I was producing for ABC News at the time and decided to do additional testing of animal psychics on ABC's watch.

"Why not get a dog psychic to try to read Diane Sawyer's dog?" I pitched the executive producer of a documentary program,

Turning Point. "It can be part of a story exploring the animal mind."[7]

I got the go-ahead and phoned Samantha Khury.

"I want you to let us fly you to New York and read Diane Sawyer's dog," I proposed in my most persuasive voice. "It's a great way to bring the idea of animal communication to a national audience."

With only a touch of hesitation, Samantha agreed. Maybe she more or less trusted me after the reading with Brio. Samantha lived in California, and after she arrived in New York we met in the hotel suite we'd booked for the event. Here, Samantha was introduced to Diane and her Gordon setter, Charlie.

Diane only briefly spoke with Samantha, as we'd planned, and gave her virtually no information about Charlie except for his name. For his part, Charlie seemed quite anxious and very attached to Diane. He kept trying to climb in her lap, almost crushing her.

"He's always like this," Diane said apologetically. "I'm afraid he's neurotic." Then Samantha and Charlie left us and disappeared into the bedroom for about an hour. When they emerged, Samantha reported what she'd learned.

"It took him quite awhile to settle down but finally he started to trust me," she told us in the calm voice of a doctor with a good bedside manner. "I wondered why he has such anxiety. He told me that when he was a puppy he remembers 'spinning,' falling downward in a spiral. That scared him."

Diane, who I think approached this venture with even more doubt than I felt at the beginning of my journey, looked startled. "He actually did have an accident when he was young," she said with surprise. "He fell into a swimming pool."

Samantha seemed to have done it again.

A day or so later, we taped another test with Samantha and Charlie—this time at Diane Sawyer's home outside of New York City. First, we shot Charlie inside and outside the house. We followed him through the dining room; we watched him outside in the big yard. Samantha was not present during this part of the taping.

She had no idea where or in what type of house Diane lived. Later we interviewed her.

"What did Charlie show about where he lives?" I asked.

"He shows me a room with a lot of furniture. He's winding around the furniture."

That sounded very like the dining room though it could have been lots of rooms. But then she reported that Charlie showed her a yard: "He says there's a lot of big trees near some water. He likes to go around under the trees."

That was a pretty exact description of the yard. We had taped Charlie under the trees and near the water that bordered the property.

Again, the results defied easy explanation in terms of the ordinary material world. This was certainly no scientific study. But the results posed more questions about how Samantha could have relayed information ostensibly from Sawyer's dog that accurately reported on both his environment and events in his life. The scene was good television. As a producer, I hadn't revealed anything to my colleagues about the personal need I had to find out if the animal psychics were for real. I was pleased by Samantha's "translation" of Charlie because it at least meant there was a possibility that she and other communicators weren't fabricating their abilities. If what she said had turned out to be patently false, I would have been disappointed. Now I realized that more than simple curiosity was at stake in my investigation. Skeptic as I was, I secretly wanted animal communication to be true.

Dog psychics generally tell clients that everyone can develop the ability to "read" a dog on some level. I didn't really believe that I could actually "hear" what Brio was thinking the way the psychics could. Yes, I could now read his body language much of the time. But when I tried to see if I could visualize a "down" or a "sit" and have Brio obey the command, nothing doing. Either Brio didn't get the picture or he didn't want to! And I heard no messages back telling me what was going on his head. I evidently couldn't access whatever frequency the animal communicators said they could tap into.

The experience with Charlie and Samantha had really whetted my curiosity. I could no longer tell myself it was a purely professional interest; it was something more. I had to keep pursuing what was now almost an obsessive need to keep investigating animal communication and testing its validity.

4

When Another Door Opens

AS MY CURIOSITY DROVE ME TO KEEP EXPLORING animal communication, I had a great advantage—my work. There was also growing public interest in the thoughts and feelings of our fellow animals—especially dogs.

So I seized the opportunity when another chance came along to do a story about animal psychics.

I pitched ABC News the idea of doing a story to see if a psychic could predict the winner of the upcoming Belmont Stakes horse race. I found Dawn Hayman, an animal communicator based in upstate New York.

I'd interviewed Dawn ahead of time on the phone. "I'm a producer with ABC News," I explained in a friendly tone. "I'm doing a story about animal communication, and we want to see if a psychic can predict the winner of the Belmont Stakes. Would you be willing to come down to the track and let us tape you with some of the horses?"

Dawn was a bit hesitant. "I've never been on television. What if I don't do it well? What if I don't get anything from the horses? I'm used to private consultations with my clients." Her doubts actually made me trust her more. She didn't seem to be bent on selling herself. She sounded articulate and thoughtful. Still, she had a gruffness. I worried that she might not be good on TV. However, she also had a quirky sense of humor that I thought might make her appealing to viewers.

"I'm not out to do some kind of exposé," I assured her. "It'll be fun. No one expects you to be perfect."

So Dawn agreed. I tried and tried to get several trainers to let her "talk" to their horses. I really wanted to tape Dawn communicating with one of the favorites in the race. But I kept getting turndowns from the trainers. They evidently thought the whole idea was nuts.

Finally one trainer agreed. His charge was the longest shot of all, indeed the longest shot in Belmont Stakes history: 70 to 1. Beggars can't be choosers, so I introduced Dawn to Sarava the day before the race.

When I first met Dawn in person I was a bit surprised. She seemed collected but certainly lacked the physical demeanor of someone made for TV. She was a bit stocky with short hair, and she seemed reserved at first, even brusque, as I'd picked up on the phone. Now that the moment of truth was at hand, I feared she'd get cold feet and freeze on camera.

The trainer Kenneth McPeek led Dawn up to Sarava's stall. Sarava had his head extended over the stall and was munching hay. Dawn stood right by him and explained to him that she was going to talk to him. We all waited for what would come next.

Sarava continued to munch hay. Dawn was completely silent. Minutes went by. The cameras rolled. I had a gut-wrenching feeling that this story was not going to be scintillating. From having watched Samantha work with Diane Sawyer's dog, I understood that Dawn was trying to "hear" what Sarava had to say. But I had expected Dawn to talk out loud more, to let us know what she was asking and what Sarava was saying as the conversation moved along. But Dawn just stood there for what seemed an eternity. This was not great television. I squirmed, imagining what the camera crew must be thinking. No doubt they concluded that they had a crazy if not incompetent producer.

Sarava's eye was quiet. He hardly moved. Eventually, Dawn pronounced out of the blue: "He says he's going to win. He wants to win and he says he can do it." I froze. I couldn't believe she was saying this on television about a horse who was the longest shot of all. How was I going to manage to save her from looking completely foolish if not a sham? Even the trainer seemed shocked. Dawn herself didn't seem nervous now; she had the aura of inner certainty.

"Why does he think he's going to win?" the trainer queried in a rather plaintive, uncomprehending voice.

"He just knows he can do it," Dawn persisted calmly. She didn't seem worried at all. "He feels good. He's confident. He wants to do it for you and his owner." I resisted the urge to laugh.

There seemed to be nothing to be said or done except to run the race the next day! As we left the track, I was still trying to figure out how I could make this story into something. It seemed to have little promise.

At this point, my inherent skepticism had again reared its ugly head. I now had few expectations of Dawn. But that other voice in my head, the one that really wanted to believe that Dawn and other psychics could tell me what Brio wanted to say to me, wasn't going to be quiet. On the taxi ride to drop Dawn at the airport I decided I might as well test her on Brio.

"Dawn, can you tune into my dog?" I asked. I was worried about him, because at the time Brio was very, very sick with a serious, potentially fatal condition called pancreatitis. He might have gotten it from eating the fat off raw bones that I'd given him, thinking it would be good for him. He had bloody diarrhea, vomiting, he could hardly walk, and he'd been hospitalized. He was also on intravenous medication. This was the first serious illness he'd had. He'd never been in the hospital. Was he afraid? Did he think I'd abandoned him there? But I'd been working and had no choice. I'd pushed my worry to the back of my mind until I sat with Dawn in the taxi.

I didn't tell Dawn about the pancreatitis or the hospitalization—not a thing.

"What kind of dog is it?" she asked, cautioning me once more about the parameters of our experiment. "I'm used to doing readings with clients in private. I've never met you before." She looked at me suspiciously. I felt she surmised that I was trying to trap her into making a mistake and that I'd say, on national TV, that she'd failed. At this moment she seemed to lack confidence—and my trust in her abilities, if not her truthfulness, waned even more.

"Brio is a black standard poodle," I told her. And nothing more. Dawn was silent, just as she'd been with Sarava. Then, after a few moments, she spoke.

"There's something wrong with his stomach, but he feels that he's in good hands. Is there a woman taking care of him? He says he likes her."

The veterinarian was a woman. I was amazed. I'd swung back toward doubt when Dawn had said Sarava would win. But this was personal; this was Brio. Dawn had no way of knowing he was sick, no way to know he was in the hospital with a woman vet. Remember, I had never met Dawn before this day. She knew me only as a TV producer who had recruited her for this shoot. I had to tell her she was right. She was not surprised. She evidently knew it.

"The first thing that struck me was how clearly he came in. I thought right away, *Wow, what a great relationship this is,*" Dawn told me with a touch of surprise. I could see she now saw me in a different way, not just as a coldly professional TV producer. Maybe I didn't want to show the softer side of myself at the time. Maybe I didn't even see it. But Dawn did—through Brio.

Dawn continued. "It's delightful for me because it's something you're unaware of. I see people more aware, some unaware. I see animals who are profound teachers, what I call deep souls or master beings, and there are people who don't get that. You know what you have in Brio, although not so much on a conscious level. But you *hear* him."

Dawn was right. I was coming to intuitively "hear" Brio, though

I wasn't consciously aware of how profound the connection really was and what Brio's true meaning in my life would come to be.

Dawn flew back home. The next day was the running of the Belmont Stakes. Despite Dawn's reading of Brio, I had very low expectations for her prediction that Sarava would win. I was still working on plan B for creating some viable story for ABC.

I watched the TV coverage from Belmont. There was a huge crowd—the biggest in Belmont Park history—and equal hype for the race. The superstar, War Emblem, who'd won the Kentucky Derby and the Preakness, was the favorite to win the race and the Triple Crown. I watched Sarava in the paddock, being saddled by his trainer. He seemed rather lackadaisical, not the image of a fired-up horse about to win a major race. At post time, as the horses entered the starting gate, there was the familiar clutch in my stomach that I always felt at the start of a race. There was also worry for the horses' safety along with the excitement of rooting for my favorite.

In truth, I felt little attachment to Sarava. I'd prepared myself to expect nothing from him. No doubt he'd live up to his predicted odds—the longest shot in the history of the Belmont. And the horses were off! Going into the backstretch, Sarava trailed behind the leaders. The announcer barely mentioned him. Into the backstretch War Emblem made a move. The excitement in the track announcer's voice fueled expectations of the Triple Crown win. "There's an inviting opening for War Emblem . . . with five furlongs to go!" The favorite moved up to battle with the early leader. "Four furlongs to go," the announcer yelled, "Medaglia D'Oro in an all-out battle with War Emblem." It looked like War Emblem might pull it out. Sarava was running fourth. Then the final turn to home. Sarava was on the move. The shock in the announcer's voice was palpable: "Sarava has come through to take the lead. War Emblem has given way . . . a huge upset is looming!" Sarava pulled to the front, past War Emblem and the other leaders. He was in front. He had won! "Under the wire! The biggest upset in the history of the Belmont Stakes," the announcer shouted.

My mouth was open. I couldn't move. How could this have happened? How could Dawn have predicted this? It took me several moments to even move. I was stupefied. Finally, I called Dawn. Both of us were almost speechless at first. The moment felt like a dream that had somehow materialized in the physical world. Dawn, presumably, was more accustomed to living with this kind of reality in which events imagined or seen in some other dimension actually occur in the material world. But even for her, Sarava's victory was stunning. She was teaching a workshop at her upstate New York farm and she and all the students had been watching the race.

Dawn's partner had low expectations: when she'd heard that Sarava was running at 70 to 1, she'd remarked, "Oh my God, they could have found you a horse with better odds than that!" Then the horses were out of the gate and were off. Dawn remembers: "All of a sudden he pulls out. He keeps going and the whole workshop is standing and screaming and yelling. I stood there with jaw dropped. Then the tears started. His heart was so in it. He understood what he was doing. He understood about War Emblem and all the hype. When he got to the finish line he knew what he had done—the pride!"

So her first reaction was happiness for Sarava. "He says he knew he could do it. He's really glad he won for his trainer and his owner."

"Did he really tell this to you?" I asked, still doubting, still wanting an explanation. "Is it possible that you had some kind of precognition of what would happen and that's how you knew, not because Sarava actually said so?"

Dawn never wavered. "Sarava told me. He was sure."

They say that we don't open to new possibilities until we hit bottom. They say that when a door closes, another one opens. The universe was about to open a new door both for Brio's well-being and for my deepening belief in the world beyond our own.

Dawn's prediction of the winner of the Belmont Stakes, and her accurate reading of Brio's illness, had pushed me further down the road toward trust in what psychics can do. Up until now though, my investigation had still been driven by curiosity; it did not seem essential. I was a journalist, a reporter, looking at my exploration of animal communication from the outside, still pretending to be somewhat objective. Then one day, when he was eight years old, Brio collapsed on the sidewalk in front of my apartment building. All of a sudden he just couldn't walk. He sat in place no matter how much I pulled. I tried to prop him up, to push him into moving. But his hindquarters folded. They just didn't work. I was frantic.

The doorman somehow helped me get him into my building and up to my apartment, where he lay down. He looked at me. He was physically paralyzed but not panicked. I was the one paralyzed with fear. I couldn't move, out of shock. My dog, who loved to prance and chase squirrels and run with the wind on the beach, was partially paralyzed. *How could this be happening? He's so young. What am I going to do? I cannot lose him.* The thoughts raced through my mind. *I have to fix him right now. I can't manage this way. What's wrong with him? I want this not to be happening.* I wasn't breathing. I felt sick to my stomach. I had to fix it. I had to fix *him*. But I—the me who always had to feel in control—*had* no control. It terrified me. It was Brio who accepted his situation, apparently with no fear. He seemed to trust that things would be all right, that they would be fixed.

I called the vet.

"Brio can't walk." I was gasping. My voice cracked. "Please tell me what to do; please help."

"Tell me exactly what's going on: How did it happen? Did he get in an accident?" the vet, Dr. Jennifer Chaitman, asked, trying to get simple information.

"No, nothing happened," I told her. "All of a sudden he just couldn't seem to move," I choked out. I wanted to not move, to just stay there with Brio. If I just remained still maybe all this would go away. It wouldn't be true.

The vet pushed me into action. "Bring him over as soon as you can and I'll look at him." So I put my arm under Brio's stomach and supported his hindquarters as I got him into the elevator. Somehow I got a taxi that would take a big dog.

Nothing seemed real, though of course I knew that Brio and I had started down some new path.

A battery of tests followed. First the physical examination—the vet found nothing broken, nothing wrong. Neither X-rays nor blood tests showed any problem. Then over the next weeks came the specialists: A cardiologist who ordered electrocardiograms for his heart. Nothing there. Then the orthopedist. He couldn't find anything. Weeks went by and no diagnosis. Then came neurological tests including an MRI scan of his spine. Finally, the verdict from the neurologist was that he had something wrong with his spine and/or neck. The diagnosis was degenerative myelopathy, a progressively disabling disease. The neurologist said that, in his opinion, Brio would most likely not regain the ability to walk properly, much less run.

All the air went out of the room. All the air went out of the world. Nothing was right. Nothing else mattered but my wonderful dog who now couldn't walk.

He's only eight; this can't be. It can't be. I lay on the floor with him—again on my kitchen floor, mulling these words over and over. Something in me just could not accept that the doctors were right, that this was it. Our active life together—running on the beach, watching him chase the seabirds and the deer and the squirrels—all of that was *over*?

Despite my experience with animal communicators, it hadn't occurred to me to call one of them. This was a serious, medical emergency. This was a situation for medical expertise, and I trusted Western traditional medicine. I had no idea that this moment would mark the beginning of the next stage in the evolution of my understanding of dog-human communication. It would drive me far down the road toward real belief in the existence of some connective thread between people and animals—between beings—that lies beyond reason and outside the perception of our five senses; a thread with immense potential to forge connections of understanding and healing.

A business acquaintance and dog person who had no idea I talked to dog psychics and was the last person I thought would consult one himself, heard about Brio. He suggested I contact an animal communicator he'd used in the past named Alecia Evans. Peter told me that Alecia not only "read" animals' thoughts, but she also did long-distance energy healing. While initially skeptical, I would learn that many so-called energy healers claim to be able to do their work without ever meeting either the animal or the human being with whom it's connected.

I would do anything to make sure Brio had a chance to live as he wanted, to run and prance and express his energy and love of the world and being in his dog body. So I moved past skepticism and doubt and a fear of feeling foolish. At my desk in my New York apartment I picked up the phone and dialed Alecia. I decided to be open to what she'd say and to how she might help.

"My dog is virtually paralyzed. The vets say he'll never walk normally again. They say there's something wrong with his spine and neck. Can you tell anything? Can you help him? I'm ready to try anything." My voice was constricted, tight with fear. When I got the words out, they were raspy and cracking.

Alecia was calm and professional, completely unemotional. She asked only for Brio's name, breed, and age. As I now expected when speaking with psychics, there was a long silence on the other end of the phone. As usual, I had to resist saying something, asking what was happening. I had to just go with it and trust that Alecia was somehow connecting, or trying to connect, with Brio. These psychic silences always unnerved me until I talked myself into just surrendering to them. Then, actually, I could feel a little peace come over me.

"I don't feel anything wrong with his back or spine," Alecia finally said. I felt weak—a mix of relief and shock. I didn't know if I believed it. Maybe she was just telling me what she knew I wanted to hear because she could sense how upset I was.

"What do you mean? The neurologist insisted there's something wrong with his spine. He had an MRI scan and everything," I blurted out before realizing that I sounded like I was calling Alecia a liar or an incompetent or both. I wanted so much to trust her, to know that she spoke the truth. But what was she saying? How could she just go against what all the skilled and trained doctors had told me? Alecia, apparently used to this kind of a reaction, reassured me gently.

"Give me a few minutes," she said confidently, not at all ruffled by my outburst. "Let me feel him and work on him a few minutes, then we can talk as much as you'd like."

Brio lay peacefully on the floor. I waited, thinking, *Now she's going to find something. She's going to agree with the vet.*

"Okay," Alecia resurfaced. "The energy wasn't flowing right through his neck and back to his hind quarters. I worked on it, and now it's flowing better. I should do some more work in a week or so. But he will get better. You're going to have your dog back."

"You mean he'll be able to walk and run?" I wanted to hear it over and over again. I couldn't hear it enough. I wanted a loop of it in my ear all day and all night.

"Yes, absolutely." Alecia explained that when she does energy work on an animal, she connects to its energy, even feels its energy in her own body. "Sometimes what happens with energy is you plug into it. I merge with his energy flow so what he is hearing is what I can hear." Despite my past exposure to the world of pet psychics, this was still hard to believe.

But over the next few weeks, Brio did improve. Alecia worked on him more, over the phone. First he was able to get up and hobble around a bit. I could take him out and he could go to the bathroom. Through it all he was stoic, and above all, valiant. I couldn't believe how valiant he was. He always tried his best. He never complained. The light in his eye, that presence, never left. If he couldn't move much he'd lie on the floor and play with me by lifting his paw and waving it at me. It made me cry. It was as if he was saying, "Don't worry. I'm still me. It's going to be alright." I thought, *He's teaching me something: if only people could be like this when things are tough. If only I could be like this!*

In another couple of weeks, there was more flow and flexibility in the movement of his hindquarters. I forced myself not to push him, not to rush things. I was afraid he'd get worse again. He was taking no medicine. I didn't go back to the neurologist. Soon he was walking quite normally. And then he was running! I couldn't believe my eyes. I could breathe again. The air had come back into the world. I'd witnessed my miracle. When Sarava won the Belmont Stakes it was someone else's miracle. But this one was all mine. It was between me and Brio and some invisible force. I didn't know what. But now, I had to believe in it.

After this experience I could no longer deny that it was within the realm of possibility to connect in some inexplicable way to another being over a distance. The word *gratitude* does not begin to explain what I felt. I had my dog back. The world felt right again. I felt whole again. And I would carry this experience—this miracle—with me forever.

I still didn't really understand how Alecia had done what she'd apparently done. It seemed Alecia couldn't really explain it either. She just knew it as true and accepted it. "I was never in your house. I never laid my hands on your dog. But you knew something was different. He was better. That's the amazing part for me: this path has allowed me to move past a lot of the barriers that I was taught as a child of how the world 'really works.' In trusting my connection to the animals," she said, "it has led me to trust what I feel in their bodies."

Alecia wasn't finished. "Brio's crisis," she said, "is opening you up to different things that you might not necessarily be open to. You're allowing yourself to be open to different awarenesses and different healing practices because you're willing to do anything to get your dog better." She was right. Had I not been desperate to help Brio and unwilling to accept the prognosis offered by Western medicine, I am quite certain I would not have looked beyond it.

Now, I was willing to try anything that offered the promise of keeping Brio healthy. Before, if someone had suggested going to a kind of chiropractor who supposedly adjusted spines without any physical touch, I would have hastily dismissed such a treatment as "New Age" hokum. Yet the suggestion from Alecia to take Brio for regular sessions with such a practitioner had me on the phone booking an appointment. It was certainly out of my comfort zone.

On our first visit, Dr. David Mehler moved his hands in the air over Brio's back. "He's some kind of king," Mehler surprisingly said. "It's like when a person knows more about the world than you do. He's just here in a dog's clothing, but he wants to be seen for who he is. I do." He continued, "Everything has inborn wisdom." In later years Mehler told me, "He saw things. He knew what he knew and what you didn't know."

It was striking that these alternative healers never acknowledged that there was anything wrong with Brio. They spoke only of who they felt he truly was. Here was yet another person telling me that my dog was an old being, a high one, in an animal's disguise. "There was nothing that he needed here," Mehler told me. "He's staying to be with you."

Mehler never offered any concrete explanation of how his treatments actually worked, except to say that he was facilitating the body's own natural inclination to heal, to work perfectly. Strange as it was, I could see results. Brio was less stiff after the sessions. I saw enough of a difference that I actually tried a treatment myself. I was stunned. I could feel my back stretch out. I felt straighter, lighter.

Brio and I continued to go to Dr. Mehler, and I also found an animal acupuncturist who gave Brio regular treatments. He always moved better, with more fluidity, after the sessions.

Over the next several years, as Brio continued to chase squirrels and run with the wind, this experience of healing with Alecia never strayed far from my thoughts. It marked the beginning of the next stage in the evolution of my understanding of dog-human communication. The physical evidence that some invisible power or energy had allowed Brio to walk and run again was incontrovertible. My experience so far with psychic mind reading was startling. But the fact of Brio's recovered physical health was something else entirely.

While I tested my own intuitive abilities a bit, I continued to use the animal communicators. I still needed translators. When I had used them for a TV production, they were not paid. But when I engaged them privately I did pay for their services. However, I continued to give them little or no advance information about Brio. Moreover, if a psychic did not give me specific information that they could not have known by ordinary means, I stopped using them. I wanted more than ever to understand what the communicators I did use seemed to be able to do. How had they come to have such seeming confidence that what they were "hearing" from an animal was true? Did they ever have doubts? If I could understand more about how they did what they apparently did, could I learn to do it myself?

I wondered what dog trainers and other experts thought of psychic communication. Had they ever had such experiences themselves? And what, if anything, is science contributing to the subject of animal communication? The search for answers led me onto the next stage of my quest to understand not only my dog, but also what I now realized was a realm beyond traditional assumptions about the world—a realm that was actively beckoning me.

5

A Dance that Becomes a Song

ACROSS A WIDE EXPANSE OF GREEN FIELD something magic is happening. On this bright sunny day in North Carolina, just cool enough to allow the warmth of the sun, a dog and a man seem bound by some invisible cord. The dog is so far off as to be nearly invisible to the man. Only an occasional command or whistle reaches through the distance between them, piercing the sound of the breeze. To an untrained observer, even *this* minimal communication is indecipherable. Yet somehow it's obvious that these two beings are truly connected in an intricate dance.

Brio's seemingly miraculous recovery had changed my fundamental bias regarding telepathy with animals. Subtly—and perhaps subconsciously—I found myself shifting from the position of curious investigator to almost-believer in the possibility that there might truly be some invisible line of communication between humans and dogs. But I needed more than my own limited experience. The insatiable reporter in me wanted to know the bigger story. First, I wanted to question animal experts about their thoughts on the subject. I also decided to seek out well-known dog trainers who were also writers. They would have thought about the relationship between humans and dogs and the ways in which they communicate and understand each other.

With some trepidation I went to meet with renowned sheepdog trainer and author Donald McCaig. Craggy-faced, crusty, and bearded, McCaig is a down-to-earth sheep farmer on his land in Virginia. I didn't know how he'd react to questions about psychic communication with dogs. He'd asked me to meet him at a sheepdog trial, and I soon saw why. He knew that having me watch the dogs and their handlers in action could explain in a way that words could not what he felt was going on.

It was spellbinding to watch as dogs and humans worked the sheep. The handlers used whistle, voice, and hand signals. Donald McCaig explained this language of the physical senses. But still the communication between species seemed somehow invisible and inaudible, deeper than hand gestures and sound. "You can't write about what's truly going on between human and dog," McCaig said. "You can't be verbal when it's not. I'm convinced that communications with dogs are very profound." He mostly spoke about the communication between the two species that we were watching in terms of art and even mystery.

Another border collie handler, Robin Queen, says of the teamwork between dog and human working to herd sheep: "Honestly, it's like magic. When it works, well it's like nothing I've ever experienced. A lot of shepherds refer to it as 'grace.' It is the epitome of grace."[1]

Queen is actually, by profession, a linguist at the University of Michigan. So she decided to look beneath what did seem to her like magic and see if it could be explained, at least to a degree, in linguistic terms. Were the dogs in fact understanding the whistles and gestures of the handler as a kind of language—an organized communication system? Did the whistles have specific meanings for the dogs? Were they able to interpret them if used with a different volume or inflection? To Queen it seemed that they could. But the research in this area is early.

Of course there is other new research on the cognitive abilities and intelligence of dogs. In Europe, a border collie named Rico drew the attention of scientists in the early 2000s when his owners said he knew the names of two hundred different objects. Researchers from the Max

Planck Institute for Evolutionary Anthropology in Germany tested Rico. In their experiments, Rico could retrieve specific objects with no clues given to him other than the objects' names.[2] A psychology professor in South Carolina, John Pilley, heard about Rico and decided to train his own border collie, Chaser, to learn words. Chaser did in fact learn to identify more than one thousand different toys and other items by name.[3]

From these and innumerable other studies it seems that we and dogs are more alike than we ever thought. This observation goes beyond the realization that dogs have cognitive and perhaps even linguistic abilities. It extends to social cooperation—like the teamwork of border collie and handler. It's been thought that a key factor that makes us human and allowed our species to survive is our social nature, our inclination to communicate with each other in order to work for a common purpose. We may be better at it than other species, but perhaps not totally unique. Out on those fields as the border collies work, it's hard not to feel that the two species are bound together by some invisible cord and to a common end.

Donald McCaig keeps returning to the idea that there is something inexplicable going on out there, something that reason and even scientific experiments cannot help us totally understand. "That kind of communication between handler and dog," McCaig told me, "is just like music, two musicians working with each other, improvising behaviors. It's a dance that becomes a song."

"So is it a kind of telepathic communication?" I ventured forth with the question.

"It's beyond rational behavior, that's for sure," came the answer that surprised me. For all the training that goes into the making of a good sheepdog, McCaig insisted that the training itself cannot entirely explain the poetry and beauty when there is perfect coordination between a handler and his dog. "There are times . . . [when] you're not in their world.

"Telepathy," McCaig continued, "is getting to a place where it's impossible to decode. The first part is training, but then it goes beyond that." He quoted an old handler who once told him, "I've never had a year when I didn't say, 'My God, I don't know much about this.'" "A good run," McCaig said of dog, man, and sheep working together, "is like being in a trance; it's like a dream."

As the day on that green field wore on, McCaig revealed more of what clearly is his conviction that human-dog communication can and does go beyond the realm of the visible and the rational. He told me about an instance during a recent winter when he sent one of his dogs to a neighboring field to retrieve a bunch of young sheep who'd escaped from their home territory. "The dog came back," McCaig said, "with a report: 'There are no sheep there.' He understood what I wanted and I understood his report. That's pretty profound stuff."

McCaig's openness to the mystery that lies within the deep bonds and understanding between some dogs and some humans contradicted my assumptions that dog trainers would tend to be very practical and wedded to training practices based on domination over and control of the dog.

Certainly, there are trainers who do not believe that the idea of telepathy explains any kind of close communication, even between humans, much less between two species. I spoke with one widely respected trainer/handler of search and rescue dogs who did not even want her name used in a book about psychic communication. She told me, "As a trainer I find [that idea] insulting because it denigrates the possibility of genuine nonlinguistic communication with the animal." This trainer does, however, strongly believe in that possibility. Search and rescue—SAR—training, she said, "is not about getting a dog to do what you want to do, but directing the dog toward a goal you mutually share, burying your ego and believing what the dog says."

Moreover, this trainer did acknowledge that there is sometimes something about the connection between a dog and a human that goes beyond explanation in terms of the physical senses—beyond verbal commands, beyond body language—beyond sound, sight, and smell.

She felt such a remarkable connection with one of her dogs, a German shepherd who was "very technically skilled." This trainer came to believe also that the shepherd dog "had a profound sense of duty and obligation" to her work. She recalls an experience when she and the dog found a man's body in the woods. The trainer "thought he would be dead from the look on his face." But somehow the dog got to him through thick rose shrubbery. She started licking the man's face; he turned out to be alive. The trainer told me that her canine partner "was a different dog from that day forward. What changed her was that she knew that she had found a human being who was not fine, who needed help."

This trainer has had several dogs and several working partnerships. She and her training partner both work with these dogs. It took the German shepherd longer than some other dogs to become fully proficient at her work. But it was clear that she was special. The trainer says her human partner "likes to joke about the spooky connection that the three of us had and this dog's ability to know what each of us was thinking. As with anyone who has a profound relationship," she told me, "it happened in a way with her that hasn't happened with any other connection in my life." That connection took place through—in the trainer's words—"genuine nonlinguistic communication."

Surely there is body language between trainer and dog. Just as surely, body language alone doesn't seem to fully explain the depth of the invisible tie between some of these trainers and their dogs. Telepathy, I was led to remember, is defined as "the purported transmission of information from one person to another without using any of our known sensory channels or physical interaction."

Bash Dibra, the dog trainer who worked with Brio initially, spontaneously brought up his belief that humans and dogs can connect on a spiritual level, a declaration I hadn't expected from a professional dog trainer. "What will happen in that spiritual communication level," Bash explained, "is it's like a special channel or airwave that opens up. It's a special language. When you create that language sometimes you think your thoughts and the dog does it." Bash went on. He, like Donald McCaig, used a musical analogy when talking about the dialogue that can occur between species. "There's something wonderful, very poetic, very musical in that bond between a human and a dog," he said. "It's like when you tune a tuning fork; you are creating music that is in harmony, so perfect, so in sync that it just flows. That's the spiritual journey of a dog and a human that can develop."

Two other renowned dog trainers and writers, Carol Benjamin and Elizabeth Marshall Thomas, also shared their thoughts on dog-human communication. Marshall Thomas, an expert on animal behavior who wrote the bestseller *The Hidden Life of Dogs,* has never used an animal communicator but tells a story that she sees as evidence of psychic communication with one of her dogs.

Some years after her daughter had been in a bad car crash and was paralyzed, Marshall Thomas and her husband went to do an errand at a shopping mall. Her husband went into a travel agency while Marshall Thomas and their dog waited in the car. As her husband came out of the travel agency door, suddenly the dog just "drooped," as Marshall Thomas put it. And she herself started crying. It turns out the person in the agency had been at the scene of the car accident that their daughter had been involved in just after it had occurred. Marshall Thomas told me, "I thought my dog was a vector. He picked up the grief and sadness from my husband and I picked it up from him. If that wasn't psychic communication I don't know what it would be."

If psychic communication does include the transmission of emotion and energetic states, then dog trainer Carol Benjamin relies on that kind of invisible dialogue every day. She has Crohn's disease, a debilitating and painful ailment of the digestive tract. She has depended on a series of service dogs to ease her pain. Often her first dog would seem to know when she was having a flare-up of the disease, even if she herself was not aware of the attack or she was trying to block it out. Her second service dog, Flash, a border collie, would ignore her denial. "I'd say, 'No, I'm fine,' then he'd keep coming back. Then I thought I should trust him,"

Benjamin recalls. "He leaned against my gut and I could feel this stuff happening, sure enough. I understood what he was doing." This is the great service that her dogs provide, Benjamin says. "By leaning against my side, the pressure, heat, and energy, plus the release of oxytocin and endorphins, will usually stop any pain very quickly."

The ability of dogs to pick up on human physical and emotional states is now widely recognized. We hear all the time about medical alert service dogs who can warn their humans to conditions such as epileptic seizures or dangerous changes in the blood sugar levels of diabetics. Some believe the explanation is a heightened sensitivity to body language, or a dog's fine sense of smell. Perhaps this is not telepathy in the strict sense of the word, meaning transmission of a thought mind to mind. But some would argue that it falls within the same spectrum of an interspecies language, transcending sound or sight. There's no strong research proving how dogs predict medical conditions.

For Carol Benjamin, this "alerting" ability of some dogs is undeniable—something that lies beyond arguing. But she also cannot argue with the fact that she herself has experienced incidents with her dogs that she cannot explain by any other means than some kind of true telepathic—or mind-to-mind communication. Benjamin had noticed that her German shepherd seemed to know intuitively when she was planning to go for a bike ride or run and take the dog along. The shepherd knew not to bother Benjamin when she was writing, but as soon as she'd think of biking, the dog would start to jump up and down.

The first few times this happened Benjamin dismissed it as coincidence. Then, she decided to do a test to see if she was actually somehow communicating telepathically with her dog. She had her sister hold the dog at the other end of her large apartment while she went into the bedroom. "I sat on the bed and closed my eyes and pictured running with the dog," recalled Benjamin. Then, almost immediately, Benjamin said, "I heard her running down that long double hallway to the bedroom, running at full speed. The dog came into the bedroom. There were two dressers with six drawers each. She went to the one that held only my running clothes and started banging on it with her nose."

Benjamin was stunned. "It actually scared me so much that I never did it again. It was too not-what-people-talk-about and too weird." Had Benjamin transmitted her thoughts telepathically to her dog? Had she "spoken" to her animal via a language that surpasses all barriers of speech?

She's had other instances while training clients' dogs when she found she could clearly just "see" something in the animal's experience or feeling that explained its behavior. Once she worked with a little mixed-breed dog that refused to walk by a staircase outside an office building in midtown New York. Benjamin took the dog to the neighborhood. She says, "Suddenly I got a movie in my head of someone picking her up and throwing her down there"—down the staircase. Once she understood this, she was able to work with the dog and ease her fear.

Benjamin believes that, as a trainer, she communicates nonverbally with her dogs through mental images. She, like many animal communicators, says that it's a visual language. "When you think about your dog, you picture the dog and the dog is getting that picture, and when dogs think of things they think in pictures and sometimes we get the picture."

Benjamin makes no claim, however, to be able to "speak" in this visual language as consistently or reliably as animal psychics claim to be able to do. "What I don't understand about the communicators is that while I've had these experiences with dogs, I can't *make* it happen. Maybe they're more sensitive," Benjamin speculates.

The idea of extrasensory perception of communication is, of course, not new. Neither is the belief that it can occur between humans and animals. It's certainly the stuff of popular imagination and myth. Consider Dr. Dolittle and the Horse Whisperer. A 2008 poll by *USA Today* found that 67 percent of pet owners say they understand the noises their animals make, and 62 percent said that they feel their pet understands them when they speak. One in five owners claimed complete mutual understanding.[4] Perhaps they are reading body language. Perhaps one can put it down to intuition. But believers in telepathic communication would argue that it's a form of intuition.

In the 1930s, the writer J. Allen Boone wrote about his relationship with the famous movie dog Strongheart. Enlisted to care for the dog while his trainer was away, Boone developed a powerful connection and way of "speaking" with Strongheart. He was convinced from the start that Strongheart could read his thoughts, even if he could not reciprocate as accurately. Over time, Boone did a great deal of inner work on himself and developed his own "invisible language" skills between man and dog. He wrote that he "had made contact with that seemingly lost universal silent language which, as those illumined ancients pointed out long ago, all life is innately equipped to speak with all life whenever minds and hearts are properly attuned."[5]

Boone would ask Strongheart a specific question. When he got the answer "it came as a 'still small voice' whispering the needed information within . . . or a sudden awareness . . . or as revealing suggestion . . . or swift enlightenment . . . or a clear direction for solving a particular problem." Skeptics will of course argue that Boone was probably just getting some kind of guidance from his own mind or consciousness.

Stories of apparently psychic animals abound throughout history. For example, in the seventeenth century there was a horse named Marocco, born in England but then taken to France to entertain in shows with his human partner, William Bankes. Marocco supposedly had amazing powers. When coins were taken from audience members, Marocco seemed to be able to identify from whom they were taken and would count the amounts by pawing with his hoof. However, as with Clever Hans, skeptics claimed he wasn't psychic after all but merely following Bankes' subtle hand gestures.[6] And in eighteenth-century London a pig and a goose purportedly could read thoughts. Today, mainstream media coverage of animal communicators and the idea that it's possible to read the thoughts of another species certainly tend toward the skeptical if not the disparaging.

Skeptics argue that psychics in general commonly use a technique called "cold reading" with humans to convince clients that they are actually tapping into their minds. In cold readings, psychics may analyze such variables as a human subject's body language, age, or dress in order to make educated guesses. Critics argue that when pet psychics work in front of a live audience, the owners' reactions let the psychics know if they're on the right track.

Linda Gnat-Mullin, a psychic intuitive who reads people as well as animals, says she herself has experienced cold readings. Once a psychic got Gnat-Mullin's own profession wrong. "I look very conventional. I don't go around wearing jangling crystals." Gnat-Mullin also thinks some communicators do too many readings and lose their intuitive accuracy because of overwork.

It's rational to assume that cold readings do happen in some psychic readings. The fact remains, however, that most of the sessions with animal communicators that I've had over the years took place by phone. I rarely gave the psychic any initial indication of whether the reading rang true. Moreover, as my investigation proceeded, I was a long way from being able to simply dismiss the idea of telepathic communication with humans or animals as hokum.

6

Multiple Sources

IN JOURNALISM THERE'S A RULE OF THUMB that one must get multiple sources to verify allegations, particularly when the subject matter is controversial. The habits of my career sent me looking for confirmation—scientific research, credible sources—that nonverbal, nonphysical communication between beings is possible, a real phenomenon. And if that were true, how might it work?

I'm no scientist, but I decided to try a small experiment myself. I designed a kind of blind study. That's the term for an experiment in which the identities of the subjects aren't known to the experimenter. The plan I devised was loosely based on this definition. Again, it made no claims to be truly scientific. *That* standard requires multiple replications of the results in tests conducted by different researchers. Still, curiosity led me on.

At my request, a veterinarian in New York City selected some dogs she had treated and diagnosed. I would give only the names and breeds of the dogs to a psychic, Alecia Evans. I also sent Alecia photos of the dogs; she had no other information. Her job was to "read" the health condition of each of the dogs. I would then check back with the vet, Dr. Jennifer Chaitman, a graduate of the University of Pennsylvania School of Veterinary Medicine and a thorough and highly regarded professional. She would say how accurate Alecia's readings were. I did not know the condition and diagnosis of the dogs. So Alecia could not read my mind. She had never spoken to or met the vet or the dogs' owners.

The results were quite stunning! There was Cassius—a golden retriever. Alecia said, "He's very sore. He does his best to keep up with his family, but he's exhausted trying to move that big body around. His left front leg and right rear leg take on most of the weight."

Dr. Chaitman confirmed, "True, he's a huge dog—116 pounds—and he has crippling arthritis."

Then there was Bo—a four-and-a-half-year-old Havanese. Alecia said that he was taking on his owners' stress and worry, and the worry weakened his own stomach energy. Dr. Chaitman wasn't sure about the worry, but again confirmed Alecia's reading of physical symptoms. "Bo had had an intestinal infection."

Moving on to Yu Tu, Alecia picked up that the dog was held most of the time and was treated like a human child—not allowed to live as a dog. Dr. Chaitman revealed that Yu Tu had a curvature of the spine and that it was hard for her to walk.

Fifi showed up to Alecia as a loving little dog but one who was "definitely in charge." Dr. Chaitman reported that Fifi often nipped her mom around the ankles!

Hobbes, a Bengal cat, seemed to Alecia to have a bacterial infection in his lungs. Dr. Chaitman had diagnosed him with an intestinal parasite with an accompanying respiratory infection!

Gracie, a Yorkshire terrier, didn't seem to Alecia to have any major health problems except for "a rear leg imbalance." Dr. Chaitman confirmed that she had had a balance problem a few years prior to our test.

When Alecia read George, another Yorkie and Gracie's housemate, she said he seemed to be developing eye issues. Dr. Chaitman said he had had one eye removed. Alecia also picked up that he had an enlarged liver. Dr. Chaitman said he'd been treated for pancreatitis.

In sum, after Dr. Chaitman saw what Alecia had reported, she said, "She is incredibly on target for almost all of them."

Dr. Chaitman says she herself has consulted animal communicators for help. "There are times when I can't figure out what is wrong with a patient after paying careful attention to the history and exploring every reasonable test in Western medicine. I appreciate how kooky this appears. But I have been amazed at how some psychics are right on target." I was struck especially by the fact that a successful, highly trained vet gave credence to the possibility of diagnosing an animal by nontraditional methods.

But how could I understand what the psychics were doing? How exactly were they working? I began to talk to the communicators I knew about their process. How do they experience what they do? How did they come to this work?

Samantha Khury said she gets pictures from animals—and also sends them. "Animals record visually," she explains. When she meets an animal, she sits very quietly in a kind of meditation. Apparently she is seeing what they're "saying" and in turn picturing what she wants to say to them. Then she translates the conversation to humans. Her clients include racehorse trainers as well as countless dog and cat owners who come to her to help solve behavioral issues.

She had so accurately described my apartment and the neighborhood where Brio and I had been living when I first went to her. "How can you do that?" I asked.

"Animals are very sensitive to their environment," she said. "And they remember things just as well as we do."

Brio once demonstrated the power of his memory in a remarkable way. I'd sold a house on the island where Brio and I often summered. It was at least a couple of years after the sale that I was renting another house there. Brio of course was with me. Some friends came to visit and wanted to see my former home. So we went—with Brio along for the ride. He jumped out of the car when we arrived at the house. Instantly he ran toward a cramped space under the wood deck that he could squeeze into. He emerged holding an old toy of his in his mouth! He must have remembered that he had left it there and known that now was the ideal time to get it. He knew we weren't living there anymore. Remarkable!

Like Samantha Khury, many animal communicators say they read animals through visual images. Dawn Hayman, on the other hand, doesn't communicate in this way. Instead, she describes "a deep knowing."

"I don't get words necessarily," she says. "I don't hear a voice, but I do get an overwhelming thought, feeling, or understanding." She considers herself to be an example of what some researchers are now calling "highly sensitive people." Studies show that about 15 percent of the population shows traits of this characteristic, including increased sensitivity to the environment and a great capacity for empathy. Biologists have also identified these characteristics in more than one hundred species.[1]

Dr. Lawrence LeShan, a psychologist often considered a pioneer in mind-body medicine, has said that "the sensitive" who has moments of apparent paranormal perception or prescience "is looking at the world in these special moments as if it were constructed along different lines from the way we ordinarily believe it be constructed."[2] In other words, they report they're seeing it from the eyes of another being or seeing things in the future beyond the boundaries of time and space.

This is exactly the kind of description that I kept getting from the intuitives and animal communicators. Linda Gnat-Mullin told me the story of a big rescue dog who'd suffered abuse and was very tense and agitated. She got pictures from the dog's point of view, she told me, of a rolled newspaper hitting his nose and a man repeatedly yelling at him. She says she told the dog that those days were behind him as she gave him a Reiki treatment. When she called the owner later to see how the dog was doing, she heard that the dog had gone into the backyard for the first time and seemed to feel much more secure.

Another time Gnat-Mullin was walking on Broadway in New York City and a dog "kind of eyeballed me," she recounts. The dog was on the sidewalk at an open-air restaurant. This time she said she got a picture of books falling from above—like big art books. "The dog looked at me very intently," she remembers, "like 'got it, got it?'" Gnat-Mullin told the owner her dog had told her a book fell on him. The reply?

"The owner looked at me and said, 'a bookcase fell on my dog!'" Gnat-Mullin says she gets pictures first, and then feelings and emotions from the animal follow.

The information traveling between animal and human, Gnat-Mullin believes, comes as vibration—information as frequency. "I think it has to do with something in the same way that our eyes are converting waves to colors and images," she explains. "I think people who can receive this have expanded their ability to receive vibrations that are subtler than vibrations that other people receive."

Lynn Younger, an animal communicator based in Arizona, also believes the connection between communicator and animal is about vibration. She says we humans seek to understand it rationally, and often end up blocking that vibrational channel over which information travels. But animals, she is convinced, "can just feel it [the vibration]." Younger told me that she often goes into a kind of trance when she's doing a reading and doesn't remember afterward what was said in the session.

I was beginning to get a sense of how the intuitives and animal communicators experienced their interactions with animals. They report feeling that they've entered a mysterious other dimension that some people seem to have a special ability to tune into—a dimension beyond the physical world of the five senses.

I played devil's advocate, looking for reasons to doubt that the psychics were truly "hearing" what animals say. I'd wondered from the start if they could be reading my mind, not Brio's. Dawn had one answer. "There is something to that. There is some part of it because you're in a relationship with Brio. So there's something of you I *can* pick up. But I can't pick up the details of how they see the world through you. Their worldview is unique to them." That reminded me again of how Samantha Khury had described my street and my apartment from Brio's perspective.

And Alecia had apparently been able to feel Brio's physical body from thousands of miles away. I certainly did not and could not do that.

I had no sense of what was going on with his spine and legs when he couldn't walk. So Alecia wasn't getting the information from me.

The communicators themselves say they've initially had to convince themselves that they truly are "hearing" the animal. Dawn Hayman initially had continual doubts. She had to be convinced by some remarkable "readings" or hunches that she got—and dismissed as mistaken—which then turned out to be true.

Dawn had an old ex-racehorse on her farm. In a dream, Dawn "heard" the mare say, "I'm pregnant and you need to feed me more." The next day, Dawn relates, the horse "told" her the same thing. Dawn didn't believe it. "I said, 'Oh, for God's sake, you're not pregnant!'"

The horse had been bred four times but hadn't gotten pregnant. One day the vet came to the farm for other reasons, and Dawn's partner told him about the mare. So he decided to do an ultrasound at no charge. "All of a sudden," Dawn remembers, "out came this laughter from the shed." The mare was indeed pregnant! The vet explained that sometimes in older mares ultrasound doesn't pick up a pregnancy. Finally, this new test did show that a foal was on the way. "It made a believer out of me," Dawn says. "I had to say, 'My God, there's something to this!'" So Dawn came to accept and believe in her apparent gift: her ability to communicate with animals.

Alecia too had doubts at first. "I grew up not believing in any of this stuff," she told me. "When I started hearing the animals, I thought, *Right, I am making this up. It's hilarious. Wow, I'm really creative and imaginative,*" Alecia said, laughing. "But then the animals would tell me things that there was no possible way I could have known. If I've never been in someone's house before, never seen the dog, I can describe the house, where the windows are, where the dog's bed is."

Once she had a client call from England about a dog that was very sick. They didn't know what was wrong. "The dog kept showing me this bag of food," Alecia told me. "I never met this dog, never saw even a picture of it. I'm just talking on the phone and tuning into the energy of the animal. The dog is showing me a bag that is purple, yellow, and orange. I asked the owner if those were the colors of the food bag. She said, 'Oh my God, yes!'" The next picture Alecia says she saw from the dog was a barn where cows were kept and where they'd be slaughtered. Then she saw rats on the floor. "I said 'Oh my God, there's rat poison in your food and nobody knows.' The dog was showing me that wherever this food was manufactured there was rat poison and the food got contaminated." The owner took the dog off the food and reported that he got better.

Alecia explains that when the animal, like this dog, gives her information, then she can bridge the gap between what they see and what they know. In this case, the dog sent the picture of the food bag and Alecia intuited that there was poison in the food. One other point about this story: it happened at a time when it was widely assumed that dogs don't see color as humans do. But Alecia was convinced that the dog was sending her the image of the colors on the food bag. Recent scientific studies have shown that dogs do in fact see color. Their color perception is more limited than that of humans. But their eyes do have color receptors, and they can use that perception to discriminate between objects.[3]

But what about other "ordinary" people, other dog people, other animal lovers? Could the average person, not trained in animal communication, feel a special intuitive, even telepathic, relationship with a dog? I also wanted to hear from people who felt extraordinary qualities in a dog or other nonhuman animal, qualities lying beyond the physical senses.

Other seemingly rational professionals reported that they felt they did have telepathic communication with their dogs. D. A. Pennebaker, the renowned documentary filmmaker, shared his experience of Bix, a large mixed breed so beloved by all who knew him that he made the pages of the *New York Times*. Pennebaker's bond with Bix led to a new understanding of dogs that changed his thinking altogether. Like me, he expected nothing extraordinary from the dog-human relationship in the beginning. He had what he calls a revelation as he came to know beyond doubt that Bix had consciousness. My conversation with Pennebaker brought a frisson of recognition. "I felt he was reading my mind," Pennebaker recalled of Bix, "and I just kind of knew what was going on in his head."

Animal communicators say that anyone can learn to "talk" to dogs and other nonhuman animals. Many people take workshops to hone their skills. There's evidence of success. Take the story of a couple of musicians in New Jersey and their dog, Shiner. Kathy and Rick Sommer had worked on communicating with Shiner. He was a rescue dog, and he had health and fear issues. They also felt he was "special," just as I did with Brio. "There was a whole deep soulful world in his eyes," Kathy told me. She and Rick even took a course in animal communication so that they could better sense what Shiner was thinking and feeling.

Then one day their communication skills became a matter of life and death. There was a car crash. Kathy was driving with Shiner in the back. The car behind her knocked into her and smashed the whole back window. Shiner escaped onto a busy highway. Kathy, unhurt but frantic, called him to no avail. It was time to test what she'd learned about telepathy. She began to send Shiner messages—images with instructions to go find a person to read his tags—and to sit and wait. Rick joined her in the desperate search for Shiner. Their tale is surely one to captivate dog lovers and help make the case for animal communication.

Kathy and Rick drove around and around in neighborhoods near the crash site, desperately looking for some sign of their dog. Finally, they got a call from a woman. She said, "I think I have your dog." Kathy and Rick rushed to the address—"the nicest block in Yonkers, New York," Kathy says. Shiner was sitting on the porch of a house— many miles from their own home, in fact in a different state—waiting. He was "waiting and watching" Kathy recalls, just as she'd told him to do telepathically. The homeowner said she'd taken one look into his eyes and said to herself, "This is an amazing dog." She couldn't tie him up, and she didn't try to get him inside. She just let him wait.

Animal intuitives certainly believe that there is an interaction between species that is unheard and unseen by the five human senses. Donna Lozito, another animal communicator I would meet, believes that all beings communicate telepathically by nature. "It's just that we humans have evolved into something different. There's too much human noise that blocks telepathic sending and receiving," she told me. Lozito—clearly led by intuition—asks, "Why do we think animals are lesser than us just because they don't speak human language? Man thinks he is the be all and the end all. When I was younger I was taught that animals don't have a soul, that they can't think and they don't have feelings."

Albert Einstein is said to have commented that "the intuitive mind is a sacred gift and the rational mind is a faithful servant. We have created a society that honors the servant and has forgotten the gift."[4] Einstein may not have said those exact words, but he wrote more than once about the importance of intuition and imagination. "And certainly we should take care not to make the intellect our god; it has, of course, powerful muscles, but no personality. It cannot lead, it can only serve; and it is not fastidious in its choice of a leader."[5]

That's one powerful voice to add to the argument that reason, our five human senses, and the material world should be seen as valuable tools—but not as our only tools, not as the only power that governs our lives.

Mainstream science has generally dismissed telepathy as actual communication between beings. From the end of the nineteenth century to the 1940s, however, there was a lot of curiosity and interest in telepathy by researchers who conducted numerous studies seeking empirical evidence of mind-to-mind communication. In the 1950s Laurens van der Post's account of his travels with the Bushmen of the Kalahari Desert triggered new fascination with the idea of telepathy. Van der Post reported that the Bushmen seemed to have an inbred ability to get information from afar; people in the camp would know when their hunters had made a kill many miles away.[6]

The accuracy of van der Post's stories was later questioned by skeptics. Some of the laboratory research in the first half of the twentieth century did show statistically positive results supporting the possibility of human telepathy. Many of the studies tested whether subjects who were strangers to each other could guess what randomly selected cards another subject in a remote location was thinking of.[7] However, often the methodology was criticized and the experiments were difficult to replicate.[8]

My blind study, along with the testimony of credible professionals, including a vet, and the psychics' own experience, bolstered my confidence. I came to think that I wasn't completely misguided in my growing belief in human-animal telepathy. To explore its validity, though, means not just studying human telepathy and ability to "read" animals but also asking the question: If animals are telepathic, can they read *us*? Can they even "talk" to us telepathically?

7

The Invisible Cord

DAWN HAYMAN, THE ANIMAL COMMUNICATOR, once told me it was Brio who'd actually convinced her to trust me after that day we met with Sarava at Belmont Park. I'd continued to check in with her occasionally to ask her to "read" Brio. Dawn said, "When I did the consultations with you, you didn't give me much feedback at all. Usually I'd be intimidated by that, but with you I wasn't, mostly because of Brio. He'd say, 'Just tell her this.' When you reacted I could feel it."

Here was the other side of animal communication—the other question. So far I'd been focusing on the humans: Was it really possible for them to know the thoughts of an animal? If so how did they do it? Now I saw more clearly, as I should have before, that if we are to really examine the possibility of human-animal communication, it's just as important—perhaps more important—to ask how animals can have telepathic connections with us. How can they understand us? How do they send *us* messages? And are those messages just about themselves—or can they be giving us information to help us, even warn us about the world around us?

A well-known naturalist of the early twentieth century, William J. Long, seems to have been the first to write about *anpsi*—an acronym coined by scientists that's short for "animal psi." *Psi* refers to "paranormal science investigation." Long assumed it was a real phenomenon, calling it "a natural gift of faculty of the animal mind, which is largely unconscious, and it is from the animal mind that we (humans) inherit it."[1]

In the 1950s and continuing through the 1960s and 1970s, a small group of scientists began to undertake experimental parapsychological research with animals. Some of these early studies were conducted in the laboratory, some with mice and rats. One focused on cats. Its goal was to see if human thought had any power to influence the actions of cats, which would indicate that the animal was telepathically "reading" people. Initial results indicated that kittens displayed above-average odds of choosing a bowl of food a human had thought of, though it seemed the closer their relationship with the experimenter, the better they did.

Follow-up studies also suggested that the closer the relationship between cat and human, the more likely the cat was to show evidence of psi in picking a cup with food in it, even when the experimenter had not actually placed the food and didn't know where it was. Thus, the cats' performance still seemed somehow to be influenced by the human relationship.[2]

As laboratory research continued into the 1970s, one focus was testing to see if animals could anticipate future events that were emotionally charged, like electric shocks or possible death. This type of experimentation dwindled after the 1970s[3]—perhaps because of growing concerns about animal rights and abuse.

While these laboratory studies have not shifted mainstream scientific opinion, they nevertheless are food for thought. Could those kittens have been linked with the humans by a kind of communications network? Even as the lab testing waned, there continued to be fascination with anecdotal accounts of animal behavior that seemed to defy explanation in ordinary terms. An instance in the 1920s was a horse named Lady. Her owner claimed she could read his mind and answer questions about numerical problems as well as past and future events if the answers were written down and shown to him. But tests didn't convince critics who saw possible evidence that Lady was helped by facial or body cues by the owner.[4]

So went the first wave of scientific attempts to prove or disprove that nonhuman animals can be telepathic.

In the early years of the twenty-first century there's been interest in a different kind of research into animal telepathy—focusing on spontaneous behavior of different species outside of the laboratory, especially when the animal has a close relationship with a human.[5] One key question has been to see if it's possible to prove anecdotal reports that dogs and other animals like cats can anticipate when their human companion is coming home or even find their person from a distance away.

That question has been studied at length by a scientist trained in all the rigor of traditional Western scientific methods. He has ventured past the boundaries of that materialistic science to explore the intuitive and extrasensory abilities of animals.

Rupert Sheldrake is a Cambridge University–trained biologist with a doctorate in biochemistry and a former research fellow of the Royal Society. He studied philosophy and history of science at Cambridge University. In his book *Dogs That Know When Their Owners Are Coming Home,* Sheldrake writes that it "is a book of recognition—a recognition that animals have abilities that we have lost."[6] Sheldrake set out to research all three of the phenomenon that fall within the term *extrasensory perception* (ESP)—telepathy, sense of direction, and premonitions—seeking empirical data to confirm and explain them.

Sheldrake's most famous case study was of a dog who seemed to know in advance when his owner was headed home. Jaytee—a terrier mix—was adopted as a rescue dog and became very bonded to his human, Pam Smart. He often was left with her parents when she went to work. The parents began to notice that he would go to the window to wait for Pam, even if her return didn't follow any set schedule. She'd leave work and arrive to pick him up at unpredictable times.

Pam Smart learned of Sheldrake's research investigating the anecdotal stories that many dogs seemed tuned in ahead of time to when their owner would be coming home. Pam volunteered to join Sheldrake's experiments. The research team started recording Jaytee's behavior over time. Sheldrake reported that Jaytee's trips to the window were closely related to the time Pam left wherever she was and headed home. On fifteen out of one hundred occasions, he did not respond to Pam's departure for home. Sheldrake speculates that he might have been distracted in those instances.

To rule out any possibility that Jaytee might have somehow been reacting to her parents' knowledge of when she left for home and their expectations of her return, Sheldrake then did experiments with Jaytee in which Pam was given random times to head for home, which were unknown to anyone else—not her parents, not Sheldrake and his team. Pam only got the times when Sheldrake and his team were not with her. This phase of the study was videotaped by a television crew.

The tapes show that Jaytee spent most of the day with Pam's parents, lying at the feet of her mother. When Pam was given a time to leave for home, the TV program showed a split screen, with one side showing Pam leaving wherever she was and the other showing Jaytee suddenly alert with his ears pricking up. Eleven seconds after Pam was told to go home, Jaytee headed to the window. The times of Pam's departure and Jaytee's actions were simultaneously videotaped by two camera crews, and the exact times of day were recorded on the tapes by the camera "clocks," or time code as it's called.

Sheldrake summarizes: "There seems no possible way in which Jaytee could have known by normal sensory means at what instant Pam was setting off to come home. . . . This experiment highlights the importance of Pam's intentions. Jaytee started to wait when Pam first knew she was going home. . . . Jaytee seemed to be responding telepathically."[7] Sheldrake conducted further videotaped experiments with Jaytee over the next couple of years, further analyzing the patterns in the data recording the dog's behavior. Sheldrake reported that "the overall pattern was similar" to that shown in the first taped experiment.[8]

The initial videotaped experiment with Jaytee triggered criticism of Sheldrake's methods and conclusions by two university psychology professors—one a well-known media skeptic. They said their own tests with Jaytee—to which Sheldrake and Pam Smart had agreed—failed to replicate Sheldrake's results. Sheldrake responded that his critics had published an analysis of only a very short time frame in each experimental period measuring Jaytee's vigils at the window. This limited measurement criterion, Sheldrake argued, didn't account for a sharp increase in the whole amount of time the dog spent at the window immediately before Pam left for home and as she was returning.

So if Jaytee did somehow know when his human had headed for home, how to explain it? Was he tuned into some information system undetectable to our human physiological senses? Sheldrake sought a theory to explain similar anecdotal stories of behavior in other species—cats, horses, and birds who seem also to know, over long distances, when their human companion is headed home. Is telepathy the explanation? *Telepathy,* as Sheldrake points out, is a word based on the Greek roots *tele* (like "telephone"—far off or at a distance) and *pathe* (sympathy)—so telepathy is "distant feeling."[9]

There are also anecdotal stories of animals who appear to have premonitions of traumatic events like death and having an uncanny sense of direction.

We've all heard tales of dogs traveling thousands of miles to find their human companions. Way back in 1923 there was the amazing story of Bobbie, a Scotch collie. He was separated from his family one summer when he accompanied them on vacation to Indiana. After having been separated from them, he journeyed all the way from Indiana back to the family's hometown of Silverton, Oregon. His determination and courage, his bond to his family—and some kind of knowledge of how to find them—took him more than 2,550 miles through territory completely unknown to him. He would have had to swim rivers and cross the Continental Divide in winter. Later, animal experts interviewed witnesses who helped to reconstruct his route.[10]

Sheldrake's studies, ongoing since the mid-1990s, have led him to believe that "telepathic communication depends on bonds between people and animals—bonds that are not mere metaphors but actual connections."[11] He writes that "the invisible cord connecting dog to owner is elastic: it can stretch and contract. It connects dog and owner together when they are physically close to each other and it continues to attach dog to owner even when they are hundreds of miles apart. Through this elastic connection, telepathic communication takes place." Sheldrake also argues that "all three types of perceptiveness . . . seem better developed in nonhuman species than they are in people."[12]

During his academic training as a biologist, Sheldrake learned of the theory of morphogenetic fields—thought to play a key role in evolutionary development. Biologists use the term to describe developmental systems within an organism. But Sheldrake thinks there is something more going on than meets the eye of materialistic science. He thinks the fields are actually fields of information linking members of a social group—a human to a dog, for instance, or animals of the same species. The information or memory of a field, Sheldrake believes, can be transferred within the group across the boundaries of space and time.[13]

I imagine these morphic fields as somewhat like invisible electrical or magnetic fields. Sheldrake says his research has resulted in a database that includes more than forty-five hundred case histories of psychic phenomena evidencing invisible bonds between humans and animals.[14]

Recently, Sheldrake also studied an African grey parrot, N'kisi, who seemed to be able to understand the thoughts and intentions of his owner and respond accordingly. N'kisi was trained by her human, Aimee Morgana, to learn more than seven hundred words and to speak in sentences. Morgana had noticed that sometimes N'kisi said things that seemed to echo Morgana's unspoken thoughts. So Sheldrake and Morgana set out to test whether the parrot really was exhibiting telepathic abilities.

The tests were set up with N'kisi and Morgana in separate rooms. They could not see or hear each other. Two synchronized cameras were set up to record them. Morgana opened sealed envelopes holding various photographs. The photos corresponded to key words in the parrot's vocabulary. Both Morgana and N'kisi were filmed, and the behavior was later transcribed separately by three independent witnesses.[15] Sheldrake and Morgana's report based on the transcriber's scoring said that N'kisi used a key word corresponding to the correct photograph more times than random chance analyses would predict. For example, when Morgana looked at a picture of flowers, N'Kisi said, "That's a pic of flowers." When she looked at a photo of someone on a mobile phone, the parrot asked, "What'cha doin' on the phone?" The results of the experiment were also analyzed by a professor of statistics in Holland. "These findings," the Sheldrake/Morgana study states, "are consistent with the hypothesis that N'kisi was reacting telepathically to Aimee's mental activity."[16]

Once again Sheldrake's methodology and conclusions came in for criticism from the skeptics.

Whether one agrees with him or not, Sheldrake is a great "character." Here is a trained scientist who has dared to step over the threshold of accepted Western scientific thought. I think of him sometimes in terms of the world of espionage, comparing him to a spy. He has dared to imagine another way of looking at the world, at the universe—at all beings. He's stepped into the mysterious unknown under the cloak of his serious empirical credentials and training. He has conducted research into animal telepathy using Western scientific methodology. He has proposed fascinating theories. I sometimes wonder if he himself has had telepathic, mysterious experiences that set him on this path. If so, like any good spy, he doesn't reveal it.

Sheldrake conducted a survey to see how many people believe that animals they've known in the past were telepathic. The survey results showed that 45 percent of pet owners and 35 percent of people currently without pets said they had known pets they believed were telepathic.[17]

But Sheldrake's mission is to find *evidence* for the belief. He wants to demonstrate that the methods of empirical, materialistic Western science can be used to investigate the invisible, nonmaterial, nonmechanistic matter of animal extrasensory perception. Whether or not he's personally a believer, he is not accepting anpsi as a given for the starting point of his scientific exploration. He's still investigating the "if" question, along with the "hows" and "whys" of animal ESP.

8
On the Far Side

AS THE YEARS PASSED, I WOULD SEE BRIO running in his dreams, legs twitching, running with the wind. I could feel his spirit; he was one with the wind, out there in some other world, on the far side, some other dimension. He was in his "teens" now—older, of course, in dog years. But inside I knew he was out there at the ocean—alive to every gust, ready to catch the breeze, always ready for what would come next.

I could see it in his eyes. He never settled, never stopped trying, never gave up, never turned away from life. I watched him, making note of his ability to savor each moment, to find joy in just being. He did not fight against growing old, did not complain of his joints or back aching, and didn't feel afraid that his time on Earth was nearing an end. During these days, he taught me about valiance and how important it is to keep playing no matter what. He couldn't walk much without help, but he would lie and wave his paw at me, just as he always had.

I kept checking in with the communicators, asking them what he was feeling. And as if Brio himself wanted me to hear what he had to say, an inexplicable, apparently telepathic incident occurred.

One day Brio again collapsed on the sidewalk in New York and just lay there, unable to walk. Within an hour, I got a call from Alecia saying she'd "heard" from Brio. When she was out on a walk, she "saw"

Brio in the clouds. Alecia said she felt she had to call me to find out what was going on. Perhaps, I thought, he had called to her for help. I asked Alecia how in the world she thought that could have happened. She remembered that there had been other times when she "heard" from Brio and felt she had to contact me. "There would be times when I would call you and ask, 'Is everything okay?' because I'd kind of get a message from Brio. It wasn't anything I was consciously thinking of, it was just because I was open to the energy. Brio found a way to allow my consciousness to recognize that he was trying to talk with me."

He was trying to talk to *her.*

Animal communicators have moved past the question of *if* animals have special abilities that lie outside the realm of the five physical senses. Even those who had initial doubts say they now believe in the profession they practice and accept animal ESP as a fact. Mainstream science is starting to accept that animals do in fact have certain kinds of "sixth sense."

There were times when I felt, without the shadow of a doubt, that Brio definitely had a sixth sense and that it was fully functional. One instance was during one of his energy/chiropractic treatments. He seemed unusually drawn to a human patient in the treatment room. He kept going over to her to sniff and sit and watch her. I wondered what was going on. David Mehler, the practitioner, said the woman had an especially "elevated" energy—very open and joyful. The woman, in the midst of her treatment, never reacted to Brio. So it was not like a normal dog-human greeting interaction. There was just no mistaking that Brio was strongly drawn to her for a reason not evident to our five physical human senses.

In the same way it appeared that Brio could read this woman's energy, animals also appear to be able to read the energy of their immediate environment. They seem to know when natural disasters are looming, enabling them to predict when an earthquake or tsunami is coming. They may be responding to subtle vibrations and tremors that are beyond the range of human perception but within their own natural biological abilities—for example, the ability to detect changes in the atmosphere or different vibrations. We know that other species certainly have abilities not accessible to humans. Dolphins and elephants, for instance, communicate with sounds not audible to the human ear.

In Brio's case, there were times when he and I were away at the beach and a large storm or hurricane was predicted. I had the advantage of weather reports in these cases. But I could have gone by Brio's behavior. A day or so before the winds picked up, Brio's attention changed. He seemed alert to every breeze, sniffing and looking as if anticipating something. I grew to expect this behavior and even to rely on it in advance of the weather forecasts.

Then there was 9/11, that day when everyone's world in New York City seemed changed forever. I was living in Manhattan, well uptown from the World Trade Center. I had to walk Brio of course. He locked his legs when we got to the front door of the building, refusing to go out onto the street. It could have been the smell from the burning towers. I believe it was also that he sensed the change in energy. There was an eerie silence—no traffic except for the sound of jet fighters overhead. Certainly my energy along with everyone else's on the street was drastically altered, shadowed by fear and panic and grief. Surely he sensed danger. I finally had to give up and eventually got him out a bit later. He himself didn't exactly seem panicked. It was as though he was saying, "No, we shouldn't go out there. Listen to me." I felt he was communicating; sending a message to me.

Margrit Coates, a well-known English animal communicator, elaborates on this sixth sense that animals may possess. In her book, *Communicating with Animals,* she writes, "Information that comes to us through our five senses frequently muffles information that is transmitted to our conscious awareness via faint and elusive wavelengths, but which is nevertheless equally important. It is through a subtle frequency that our intuition operates, and this is our sixth sense. The sixth sense frequency is received by animals more clearly than by humans, owing to our dependence on gadgets and verbal language."[1]

Linda Gnat-Mullin, the intuitive, brings up the matter of quantum physics when she tells me what she thinks is occurring when she picks up information from another species—even over the phone. "It's the non-locality of events first and foremost."

Non-locality refers to the theory of interactions—say between particles—that seem to occur at a distance.[2] Some physicists believe that non-locality thus allows objects to know each other's state even when separated by long distances. The great Swiss psychiatrist Carl Jung cited synchronicity as an explanation of the paranormal. His theory of synchronicity argued that events may be connected by meaning— "meaningful coincidence"—and are not necessarily the result of cause and effect.[3]

Non-locality, of course, is also a quality of Sheldrake's proposed "morphic" resonance theory. Sheldrake proposes that the social bonds both *among* species and *between* species are social fields that hold collective memories—like Jung's collective unconscious concept. Memory and other information is transferred, Sheldrake believes, across space and time.[4]

Today scientific research is delving into communication—and not just among mammals or even just between other animal species—but between other types of living organisms, such as trees! There's new research showing that trees actually communicate with each other in ways that had been previously unknown.

Suzanne Simard, a forest ecologist, and her colleagues at the University of British Columbia recently discovered that trees and plants actually send messages to other trees of their own species. She found a web of underground fungi connecting to the trees and plants of an ecosystem. Many of the fungi help nourish the tree roots, and experiments showed that the fungi actually move carbon, water, and nutrients between trees as needed. Older trees, for example, can use the fungi network to help younger trees.

And there's more. Scientists say that trees send electrical signals to other trees through their roots. These signals can warn of trouble— for example, a creature that's chewing on the tree roots.[5] So the trees, according to these studies, have formed a social bond with their relations and are using a communications network to help each other. Here again, we hear about "a social bond" as the foundation for communication.

How remarkable! If trees and plants can communicate this way unbeknownst to human recognition, then why should we not believe that other species can do that too? Perhaps these communications among trees can be explained purely in terms of biology. But intuitives and others who believe that extrasensory communication between living beings is certainly possible, if not a fact, argue that among all life-forms there is an interaction that is extrasensory—that is, unheard and unseen and beyond the five senses of human beings.

Joan Grant, a well-known clairvoyant and twentieth-century author, said that she was not interested in blind faith or blind belief. She argued that you must develop the five senses before you attain the sixth.

But for some, the point is that we humans often become too reliant on those physical five senses, shutting off access to a sixth sense.

Donna Lozito, another animal communicator I would meet, believes that all beings communicate telepathically by nature. "It's telepathy," she insists. "Plants communicate plant to plant. Animals communicate animal to animal. Most humans have interrupted that natural process."

What is striking is that there's clearly a movement under way—a growing urge to connect with other living beings. It's driven not only by committed believers in interspecies telepathy, but by scientists as well. Did you ever imagine a dog in an fMRI machine having a brain scan? Well it's happened! A neuroscientist at Emory University in Atlanta, Gregory Berns, wanted to find a way to see brain activity that could give clues to what dogs are thinking and feeling. To me, his decision to devote his professional skills to this exploration held echoes of my own journey with Brio. He says he was inspired by the death of his favorite dog, Newton, a pug. "I thought about him a lot," Berns told Claudia Dreifus of the *New York Times*. "I wondered if he'd loved me, or if our relationship had been more about the food I'd provided."[6]

This was exactly the question that had set me on my own journey. Of course, Berns could actually *perform* scans of dogs to seek empirical evidence of what was going on in their brains. So he trained selected dogs for months so that they would be comfortable in the scanner and able to stay still. Over the past five years, he and his team have scanned about ninety dogs with no restraints and no drugs. One experiment was designed to see what gave dogs pleasure.

The scans focused on the rewards center of the dogs' brains, comparing the activity when they were given food and when they were given praise. Most responded equally to the two rewards. But about 20 percent responded more strongly to praise. Berns's conclusion? Most dogs love their humans just as much as food—and some love us even more. Berns also discovered that dogs are born with a dedicated part of the brain for processing faces. So when our dog looks at us with that intense stare, it's their way to see what's going on with us, to connect with us, and build the bond between us. Berns says, "When you look at [dogs'] brains, you realize how similar some of their processes are. You recognize that they are not just things."[7]

Other researchers are working to decipher other "languages," or communication systems, of other species—to understand them. In past years, there have been well-known research studies that tried to communicate with animals by teaching them human language. There was Washoe, the female chimp who became the first nonhuman to learn American Sign Language. There was Kanzi, another chimp, who learned to use a keyboard showing images to represent human words.[8]

And dolphins as well are known to be highly intelligent and capable of understanding artificially created languages. There were well-known studies aimed at teaching them to communicate using English—for example, the controversial research of neuroscientist Dr. John Lilly in the 1960s.[9]

But now one dolphin researcher, Denise Herzing, uses an underwater mobile communication system to try to translate human language into "dolphinese." Dolphins communicate, and whistles and Herzing's

CHAT system are designed to allow dolphins to ask things—to talk to humans. It's two-way communication.

Herzing says, "Interspecies communication happens every day between many species: between plants, nonhuman animals, and between nonhuman and human animals. What seemed to be lacking was our acceptance of our interdependence and mutual interactions with the natural world."[10]

Herzing started researching two-way communication with dolphins in 1997. At first, the researchers used human-created whistles and taught the meanings of the whistles to the dolphins. It was hoped that the dolphins would then mimic the "whistle words"—for example, to ask for a toy they wanted. Still, all of those efforts were using a human-created "language" to try to communicate with the dolphins.

But here's the really exciting part. Herzing and her team are also putting the natural dolphin whistles into the CHAT computer. It's hoped that ultimately the system will let humans decode the dolphin whistles and find out if they really have a language. If so, think of the possibilities! What if we really *could* have a conversation in the language of a dolphin, or a chimp, or a dog? Then we could ask if they really can read the mind of a human, "hear" or "see" messages from an animal communicator, and how a dog knows his human is headed home.

As Denise Herzing says, "Imagine what it would be like to really understand the mind of another intelligent species on the planet."[11]

There's a remarkable instance of dolphin-human communication that has developed spontaneously to serve a common purpose. It does not depend on any formal translation system of audio language. Consider this: On a river near Mandalay, Myanmar, Burmese fishermen rely on Irrawaddy dolphins to help them make a catch. It's a partnership that's been going on for generations. When a fisherman taps a teak dowel against the hull of his boat, the dolphins come. They evidently know there's a job to be done. The dolphins then signal where the fish are. They do this by turning upside down, lifting their tails out of the water and slapping them down where the fish are. Then the fishermen cast their net. The dolphins catch any escaping fish. This is one of the few confirmed examples in the world of cooperation between humans and wild animals.

Consider this and ask how this communication happens. The dolphins certainly hear the drumming on the boat's hull. But how did they figure out what the fishermen wanted? How did they decide to use their tails to point to the fish and conclude that the humans would understand in turn? Do these human-dolphin interchanges involve intuition, telepathy—some kind of invisible, extrasensory means of understanding each other?[12] To me, it's a question that begs to be asked.

I sense that a growing number of scientists also feel there may be something undetectable that lies beyond the reach of their current research tools.

This is a book about dogs, but the anecdotal stories about other nonhuman animals echo and seem to support the reports about canines exhibiting apparently extrasensory abilities and behavior. Those reports are echoed by observations of other species—not just domesticated animals, but also whales and dolphins, for example. There are stories—many from researchers—of killer whales rescuing dogs from drowning and escorting them back to their people and of whales and dolphins apparently warning humans of trouble and saving them from harm's way.[13]

I believe some scientists feel they cannot speak openly about their belief—or even their hunch—that nonhuman animals have telepathic abilities. One well-known dolphin scientist is an example. She told me off the record that she has experienced behavior by dolphins that she cannot explain by any means except some kind of extrasensory perception and/or telepathic communication. Yet she will not say that for fear of risking her scientific and academic reputation.

Beyond the anecdotal observations of researchers, I've noticed another thread running through the "unofficial," untested—yes, *intuitive*—observations of a number of scientists working with a variety of nonhuman animals. It's about some kind of awareness, a "knowingness." For example, here's what Ken Balcomb, senior research scientist at the Center for Whale Research on San Juan Island, Washington, had to say about the killer whales—orcas—that he works with.

"I've sometimes come away," Balcomb told conservationist and author Carl Safina, "with a real 'wow!' feeling, like I'd just seen something above and beyond. When you lock eyes with them, you get the sense that they're looking at *you* . . . It's . . . like they're searching inside you. There's a personal relationship that they set up with eye contact."[14] Balcomb distinguishes that whale "look" from that of dogs. But when I read his words, I instantly recognized what he was talking about. I'd seen that gaze from Brio—that searching look that said, *I know you. What are you thinking? How are you? What's going on with you—really?*

There is actually research indicating that there's something that's also special about the intent stare of a dog. One distinct difference between wolves and dogs today is that dogs look at our eyes. Wolves do not. At Eotvos Lorand University in Budapest, researchers did a study showing that even tamed wolves would not initiate eye contact with humans, even though they'd been raised by them since puppyhood.[15]

True, this may not be ESP or telepathy. Perhaps it's a biological trait that evolved in dogs to help them connect to us. But that "wow!" that whale researcher Ken Balcomb felt when looking into the eye of a whale and the thrill of some essential realization that Brio's gaze awakened in me still seem to be telling us something very profound and very essential about these fellow beings.

There's something behind the gaze of nonhuman animals that gives us a frisson—a shiver—of recognition, that lets us know that there is something in that being that is offering what even another human being, even the closest person in one's life, cannot offer. That gaze seems to know things we do not know. And it seems to offer to share its knowledge—if we are open to receiving it.

Leonardo da Vinci remarked on that wisdom in our fellow creatures when he wrote, "Man has great power of speech, but what he says is mostly vain and false; animals have little, but what they say is useful and true."[16]

With all the current research into communication with animals, it seems that at least some scientists are opening this door—a bit. Perhaps ESP and telepathy still lie beyond the realm of acceptability to most researchers. But the stunning amount of new studies looking at animal cognition, emotion, and intelligence surely indicates that there's a desire to explore what is behind that gaze.

Science might just be heeding the words that nature writer Henry Beston wrote in the early years of the twentieth century. "In a world older and more complete than ours, animals move finished and complete, gifted with extensions of the senses we have lost or never attained, living by voices we shall never hear. They are not underlings; they are other nations, caught with ourselves in the net of life and time, fellow prisoners of the splendor and travail of the earth."[17]

I know one thing: That gaze of Brio's is one I shall never forget. It's the look I call when I'm in trouble. It's the look I hold in my mind's eye when I need to feel peace and harmony, and when I need to feel safe.

9

Something behind the Eyes

WHEN ONE FEELS A CONNECTION WITH ANOTHER BEING—human or dog or another sentient being—one has a sense of their emotions and how they're experiencing themselves in the world. We get an idea of who they feel themselves to be. I had certainly come to know Brio and how he saw himself. He obviously never doubted who he was. From that first day I met him as a tiny puppy waving at me, to when he trotted out onto the New York City sidewalks, to his strong spirit that never wanted during illness, he showed utter confidence in himself. Nothing and no one could diminish or defeat him. I think it was that clarity of self-knowledge that so many people recognized in him. He was always present within himself and in the moment he was living.

Once I took Brio sailing on a friend's boat. He'd never been out to sea. He had to get into a dinghy for the trip from the dock and then jump up onto the sailboat. No problem. Then he sat beside me in the cockpit as we took off, happily smiling into the wind and riding the waves like a veteran as the boat heeled over. He was in his element—as he always seemed to be! There's no other word for it: he had that presence—consciousness of himself—fully at home in his own skin as well as the living moment.

Any belief that our fellow animals are able to communicate tele-pathically or through some extrasensory ability must rest on one assumption—that they have consciousness.

Many philosophers have grappled with the concept of conscious-ness over the centuries. What is it? How do we define it? There is still no conclusive agreement about the nature of consciousness—human or otherwise—although it's generally accepted that a defining characteris-tic or prerequisite of consciousness is awareness. That means awareness of the surrounding world and awareness of other beings. It's about expe-rience and feeling. But is it purely a creation of the physical brain? Is it *just* about neurons processing information?

Neuroscientists wrestle with theories and struggle to find evidence for those theories. Does consciousness derive from something else? Or is it something fundamental, something that just *is*? The debate contin-ues with no conclusion. As Christof Koch, a well-known consciousness researcher and neuroscientist said, "I am conscious. Any theory has to start with that."[1]

Recently, there's been mounting interest among scientists want-ing to conduct empirical studies examining the intelligence, cognitive abilities, memory, and emotion of nonhuman animals. Some of these studies have been noted in earlier chapters. There's the study by the Comparative Ethology Research Group in Hungary (referenced in chapter 3) that found dog and human brains lit up in similar locations when they heard emotional sounds—crying or happy barks or human laughing.

Also, there are the dog brain scans done by neuroscientist Gregory Berns of Emory University (referenced in chapter 3 as well). These too indicate that dogs have emotion. There's the booming research field studying animal cognition and intelligence, with the amazing evidence that dogs can learn the names of hundreds—even a thousand and more—objects, and show that they're able to use the names in short sentences.[2] These are only some of the recent studies. Many more are ongoing.

The concept of awareness—consciousness—goes beyond experience of the outside world and other beings. It also refers to self-awareness, experience of what's going on inside us and a sense of our true identity. The classic research test for self-awareness is the mirror test—that is, the ability to recognize oneself in a mirror. Chimps can do this. Dogs cannot. So because of that finding, it was believed until very recently that chimps have the ability to recognize themselves but that dogs do not. In 2001 it occurred to Marc Bekoff, Professor Emeritus of Ecology and Evolutionary Biology at the University of Colorado, to see if researchers were testing dogs for the wrong sense. What if we were to test dogs for self-recognition using the sense for which they're known to be naturally skilled—smell?

Bekoff tested his own dog and others over a number of years to record the time they spent sniffing their own urine and that of other dogs. The results showed a clear ability to tell the difference between their own urine and that of other dogs.[3] That certainly showed that dogs know their own smell as distinguished from other dogs' smells. But did they truly know their own identity?

Just recently, Alexandra Horowitz, a professor at Columbia University and researcher at Barnard's Dog Cognition Lab, decided to try to answer that question. Can dogs truly recognize themselves as *beings,* as *selves?* The study found that the dogs spent more time sniffing canisters in which a strange smell had been added to their own urine than they did smelling their own urine alone. To a scientist, this means that the dogs could tell the difference between the smell "image" of themselves alone and the modified scent. Hence—self-identity.[4]

New research has also indicated that self-awareness—consciousness—exists, through tests done of how a dog's memory works. A study by the Family Dog Project at Eotvos Lorand University in Budapest, showed that dogs have memory that goes beyond just remembering a command or the name of an object. They have what's called episodic memory. The scientists tested dogs with so-called do-as-I-do training, in which they learn, when prompted by a verbal cue, to imitate a trainer's specific action. But the dogs turned out to be able to imitate the trainer's behavior even when it was something brand new and when no verbal commands were given. What's more, the dogs in the study could remember and imitate the humans' actions up to an hour later. They could relive the experience in the same way that people do.[5] That experience was taking place in their inner awareness.[6]

Studies with other species are also finding evidence of consciousness in nonhuman animals. In addition to working with the brain scans of dogs, neuroscientist Gregory Berns performed brain scans of stranded sea lions to see what might have caused the spatial disorientation they were experiencing. He found that there was damage in the hippocampus. In humans with temporal lobe epilepsy, that's the same area of the brain that's damaged. Berns found this comparison significant. "The sea lions taught me that consciousness disorders in animals can look very similar to consciousness disorders in people," he told Claudia Dreifus of the *New York Times*. "In fact," Berns has concluded, "the aggregate of my research has made me realize how similar many animals are to us."[7]

All this research on the feelings and understanding of dogs and other nonhuman animals does lead to the conclusion that other species possess consciousness. In 2012, a group of scientists gathered for the conference "Consciousness in Humans and Nonhuman Animals." They then signed the Cambridge Declaration of Consciousness in Nonhuman Animals, which stated, "Convergent evidence indicates that nonhuman animals have the neuroanatomical, neurochemical, and neurophysiological substrates of conscious states along with the capacity to exhibit intentional behaviors. Consequently, the weight of evidence indicates that humans are not unique in possessing the neurological substrates that generate consciousness. Nonhuman animals, including all mammals and birds, and many other creatures, including octopuses, also possess these neurological substrates."[8] Modern Western science is, of course, coming late to the game with efforts to unravel the nature of consciousness.

And then there's the matter of soul. Brio's quality of presence certainly spoke to his awareness of himself and the world around him. But there was more. There was that quality that others saw in him—a knowledge that seemed to reach beyond this earthly moment, into a different dimension, a consciousness of another realm. Some call this the realm of spirit or soul.

If a being has consciousness, does that mean it has a soul? Does a soul survive only in this earthly life—or forever? These questions stymie the human intellect when it seeks evidence to support one answer or another. Still, when we look to ancient cultures and religions we find specific details about the soul and whether it survives death.

The original name of *Egyptian Book of the Dead,* a funerary text used from around 1550 BCE to around 50 BCE,[9] was actually *Book of Coming Forth by Day* or *Emerging Forth into the Light,* then mistranslated.[10] It was a collection of texts that put forth ideas about the immortality of the soul that had arisen much earlier in Egypt—in the period around 3000 BCE.[11] The text lays out the detailed stages or spells of how the soul journeys through the afterlife.[12]

In India's Hindu scriptures, the Katha Upanishad also asserts that the soul exists and endures—although it cannot be seen and remains mysterious.[13]

The Bardo Thodol, known in the West as *The Tibetan Book of the Dead,* provides a guide to experiences that the soul—or consciousness— has after death. The bardo is the interval between death and the next life.[14]

For those guided completely by inner conviction—like many philosophical and religious leaders—pure belief trumps any need for justification beyond referencing the religion's historical texts. Nevertheless there is wide disagreement within philosophical and religious thought—and even within a single faith—about whether animals are feeling, thinking beings with consciousness and even souls.

Consider Christianity. It's often believed today that the Bible and later Christian texts actually supported human domination over animals. Genesis 1:26–28 (King James version) does in fact state:

Then God said, "Let Us make man in Our image, according to Our likeness; let them have dominion over the fish of the sea, over the birds of the air, and over the cattle, over all the earth and over every creeping thing that creeps on the earth." So God created man in His own image; in the image of God He created him; male and female He created them. Then God blessed them, and God said to them, "Be fruitful and multiply; fill the earth and subdue it; have dominion over the fish of the sea, over the birds of the air, and over every living thing that moves on the earth."

Here these creatures are clearly viewed as inferior to humans. There is no consideration of possible intelligence, emotional capacity—and consciousness—comparable to ours.

Also, the philosophy known as "The Great Chain of Being," which ran through Western thought from the Middle Ages into the latter part of the eighteenth century, argues that there is a hierarchical structure of all matter of life—with humans above other animals.[15]

This view of dominion over animals—according to some interpretations of Christian doctrine, was a notable shift from the view of animals in earlier civilizations. Consider the texts of ancient Egypt—from the Old Kingdom (the third millennium BCE) forward. One such text was the Forty-Two Questions, which called for the soul of the person who had just died to answer in all honesty the questions of forty-two spiritual assessors (deities) who each asked one question. The answers reveal whether they were following ethical and moral principles according to the doctrine of the goddess Maat—personifying concepts of truth, harmony, and morality.[16] Their answers determined how they would proceed on their spiritual journey.

Translations of the Forty-Two Questions vary.[17] But question forty is often translated as a mandate to care for animals: "Hast thou remembered the brethren of the Earth, and been compassionate to those younger brethren who serve thee as beasts in the field and home?"[18]

"Brethren of the Earth" refers to animals.

Question forty-one also addresses the treatment of animals. Sometimes it is translated as "Hast thou ever worked man or beast beyond its strength in greed?"[19]

Another translation by the twentieth-century English clairvoyant and writer Joan Grant is "And the forty-first shall say: Hast thou to all animals as thy master is to thee, using wisdom, kindness, and compassion unto them who were once thy brothers?"[20]

The Egyptians ate meat and used domestic animals in their work. But they revered these fellow beings and believed they had souls that had an afterlife and that they possessed spiritual equality with humans in this life. These beliefs were reflected in how they honored animals in death. Many were mummified. Some mummies were placed in decorated cases—like a large cat in a case with the title Osiris–the Cat. Osiris was the god who ruled the afterlife. The Egyptians did worship individual animals as incarnations of certain gods. And there was a touching discovery when Osiris–the Cat was recently put through a CT scanner. Its front paws were crossed, just as a human mummy's hands would be placed.[21]

To return to Christian doctrine regarding our fellow creatures, there are those who argue that a more complex view of the nature of nonhuman animals and their rights can be found in Christianity. Passages in the Bible draw from the pastoral culture of its time, incorporating a concept of nonhuman animals who could be used for human purposes but nevertheless respected and cared for. The Hebrew scriptures especially focused on the responsibility of stewardship for animals, even if they were used for human purposes. For example, King David's care for his sheep was a sign of his worth as a leader (1 Samuel 17:35; New English Bible).

Other passages champion care for our fellow animals as a metaphor for divine love.

> For these are the words of the Lord God: Now I myself will ask after
> my sheep and go in search of them. As a shepherd goes in search of

his sheep when his flock is dispersed all around him, so will I go in search of my sheep and rescue them no matter where they were scattered . . . I myself will tend my flock, I myself pen them in their fold, says the Lord God. I will search for the lost, recover the straggler, bandage the hurt, strengthen the sick, leave the healthy and strong to play, and give them their proper food. (Ezekiel 3:11–17; New English Bible)[22]

Then there was St. Francis of Assisi, known as the patron saint of animals, who tamed the wild beasts. In one of his prayers he held that our duty toward our "brethren"—animals—goes even further than just stewardship of creatures who serve us.

> *Not to hurt our humble brethren*
> *Is our first duty to them, but to stop there is not*
>   *enough.*
> *We have a higher mission:*
> *To be of service to them whenever they require it.*[23]

These words of St. Francis, reflecting his deep understanding of our fellow animals and his compassion, are words that I hold in my heart. I aim to serve the mission that St. Francis defines.

But back and forth we go when looking at Christianity's view of animals. St. Augustine argued that man has no duties toward animals except to make sure that any harm to them doesn't cause a financial loss to their owners.[24] He quoted Genesis: "Everything that moves and lives shall be meat to you."[25]

Liberal Protestants hold the general view that nonhuman animals have souls. There's no consensus though on whether they have an afterlife. Evangelicals do not believe that our fellow species live on after physical death.[26]

Judaism too reflects some ambivalence regarding animals. It's generally held that nonhuman animals have souls—but souls as defined in terms of life force. The spiritual concept of *soul* is reserved for humans. There's no idea that nonhuman animals have eternal life.[27] But it's also true that while the Torah accepted the slaughter of wild animals so long as the animal's blood was buried, rabbinic interpretation strengthened laws regarding animal welfare. And Judaism's Kabbalah mysticism, as well as orthodox Hasidic ideology, proposes the idea of the transmigration of souls; that is, that the souls of human sinners need to rise again through other beings—plants and nonhuman animals—before regaining human life. So a cow that is slaughtered in an improper manner may embody the soul of a human.[28]

In Islam, it's generally believed that nonhuman animals do have souls, though opinion differs on whether they have an afterlife.

Buddhists do believe in the eternal life and rebirth of all beings. Robert Thurman, the renowned Buddhist scholar at Columbia University, points out that the great French German theologian and humanist Albert Schweitzer, who was "very Christian," believed strongly that Jesus Christ never intended to say that nonhuman animals have no soul. Schweitzer, Thurman reports, really objected to that idea in Christian theology.

The clairvoyant Joan Grant once expressed a similar conviction. She was asked if animals are precursors of human beings or separate beings. She answered:

> The soul of an animal is just as much of God as the human being and very often much more so, because the only way one can judge the value of any particular stage in one's journey is its closeness to the divine pattern of evolution. So Eloise [her dog at the time] is much closer to the Deity than most people one will ever meet who are envious or jealous or miserly. If Christ were in the room, he would recognize Eloise as part of himself very much more easily than he would recognize some miserly tycoon, because they would have much more in common.[29]

Robert Thurman tells what he calls "a Buddhist shaggy dog story." It's a story about Maitreya, seen in Buddhist tradition as a bodhisattva— a being who seeks Nirvana and is on the path to becoming a Buddha but remains on Earth to help others. Thurman explains that the name Maitreya "comes from two words in Sanskrit—*Mater* or *Mother,* and also *friend.* Maitreya means 'altruistic love,' the loving Buddha coming in one hundred thousand years or so." In the meantime, Maitreya can manifest in many different bodies.

So here's the "shaggy dog" tale. "There's a very famous story," Thurman recounts, "about a man who wants to have a vision of Maitreya who's believed to dwell in a heavenly place until coming to Earth. So this man wants to search for him. The man tries for years and is despairing. Finally, one dark night, the man saw a bedraggled, sick dog by the side of the road.

"He decided to do something about it," Thurman continues, "and the dog turned into Maitreya. The man bowed to Buddha. He'd been trying to see him for twelve years. He said, 'What took you so long?' Maitreya replied, 'It wasn't until now that you had genuine compassion to treat a dog well and help to heal him. So I am the Buddha of love and you can see love when you have compassion.'"

So, Thurman says, the story is about the way Maitreya emanates as dogs in the world to demonstrate compassion and love. The tale of Maitreya as a dog continues to influence Buddhist treatment of dogs. For example, Thurman told me, "Tibetans really love their dogs. In Tibetan monasteries they kept a lot of stray dogs. They cared for them and tried to feed them. They were horrified when the Chinese came in and started eating the dogs."

I heard another shaggy dog story about dogs and the soul. This one began in Nepal, where Hindus also believe that nonhuman animals have soul and that every human being has already existed as other forms of life. The story came from Lynn Moore, a life coach and dog lover. Some years ago, she was living in Nepal and teaching at a monastery. Every day she would walk from her guesthouse to work, past an area where there were stray dogs. One day she noticed one very thin, scraggly looking dog. "Even though I'd seen many abandoned dogs," Moore told me, "this one caught my attention. She happened to look up at me, and there was something about her eyes in her very skinny body. She looked at me and I thought, *Oh my God!*"

Here again—there's that gaze from a dog who somehow seems to see inside one. Moore couldn't get the dog out of her mind. The next day she saw her again, shivering in the rain. "Again, my heart broke. That night I couldn't sleep," Moore remembers. "Next morning I said, 'Okay. I did it. I'm supposed to take her home.'"

So she looked for her and at first couldn't find her again.

Finally, the little dog appeared. Moore sat down next to her. The dog had a rash and fleas and might have had rabies so Moore just gently touched the pad of her paw. She found a cardboard box and managed to get the frightened dog into it with the help of a friendly passerby. She got a taxi and took the dog to a vet who cleaned her up and gave her shots. Back to Moore's guesthouse they went.

"We've been Velcroed together ever since," Moore says. "It was a wonderful, wonderful experience. She's a very calm dog, quiet, extremely loving, a very old soul. She knows exactly what I'm saying. It's hard to describe. I know I saw her soul when she first looked at me. I would say she entered my heart. That's why I could not leave her there. Sometimes I discover that when it comes to an intuition from the universe, I can reason myself out of it, but the universe was not going to give up. I said, 'Okay, I'm doing this.'"

Moore had had other dogs before, and had close relationships with them—but nothing like her connection to Atma, as she named the dog she met in Nepal. In Hinduism, *atman* refers to the personal soul or self.

There's a common thread in these stories of people who feel they've met their "soul dog." It's something set apart from close relationships they've had with other dogs, something beyond the bond they've felt in those cases. The recurrent experience one hears in these stories is that the person felt in meeting their soul dog that there was a sense of being thunderstruck by an instant and very deep connection.

I began to notice other similar relationships around me. Early on summer mornings on Martha's Vineyard, when dogs and their people walk on the beach, it was beautiful to observe their bonds. One that I noticed in particular was the close tie between Alison Oestreicher and her border collie, Sen.

Sen had initially belonged to Alison's ex-boyfriend, and when Alison had initially met this dog, she told me, "I immediately felt a connection but I don't really know what it was. His breed is a very connecting kind of dog. I was also in a very present place. I was very present with him." Then their relationship took a turn that revealed how deep it actually was. First, Alison was in a motorcycle accident and broke five bones. When she was recovering, Sen would come lie with her. "He helped me by just being with me. I was in so much pain," Alison remembers. "He just knew. People say that, but I swear he followed me everywhere. He jumped on the bed and hung out with me. He put his head on my chest and would stare at me, things he hadn't done before."

Then, sometime later, it was Alison's turn to take care of Sen. He was hit by a truck and suffered near-fatal injuries, necessitating several surgeries to save him. It was a long recuperation. Alison had left her boyfriend, but moved back in to care for Sen. "He couldn't walk. It was really harrowing. I had to figure out how to cheer him up," Alison told me. "I would do things with my hands—signals. I'd throw the ball in the air. He would follow it with his eyes. That's all he could do."

Sen's rehab took three months, and he and Alison have rarely been apart since. She fought to get legal ownership of him. They go everywhere together, and she almost never leaves him alone at home. "Sometimes I think I can read his mind. I feel like I think like Sen. I don't know where I begin and he stops." Those words of Alison's are those of a person who recognizes her soul dog.

It happened to animal communicator Cindy Brody too—that inner knowledge of a powerful connection. One December day Brody got a phone call from a woman who knew of a man whose daughter had died of a drug overdose. He was temporarily keeping his daughter's dog in his barn. He wasn't sure what to do. He had heard about Brody and wanted her to come assess this frightened pit bull. His family had suggested that he put the dog to sleep. But he believed the dog deserved a second chance.

Brody went to meet Cuddles, as the dog was then named. She was in a barn stall, her tail wagging out of control when Brody went up to her. Brody heard: *Help me! Please let me out! I'm scared! Help me! Please help me!* With that plea, and after she'd seen the dog's sweetness, Brody was able to secure placement for Cuddles in a pit bull rescue.

On the next day, Brody went to pick her up from the barn. Again, she heard the dog speak: *I'm going home with you. PLEASE!!! I'm good. I love you! Don't leave me! Let's go!* Brody already had two dogs at home and thought she wasn't in a position to take another, although her heart went out to Cuddles.

She took her first to a veterinarian to be spayed and several hours later returned to pick her up. The vet said, "You're not going to take her to the rescue tonight, are you? She could really use a couple of days in a quiet environment. She's such a nice dog." The vet continued, "I would keep her if I could."

Brody says, "I swear I saw that dog wink at the vet."

So they headed home. Within minutes of arriving, Brody found her husband and the dog—who she would rename Lilly—spooning together on the floor. That was that. The connection had been made—as Lilly apparently knew it would be.

Soul dogs—soul animals, however they may appear to us—make themselves known not through our five human senses and not through reason and intellect. We recognize them in ways we ourselves often cannot understand. We feel them; we sense their presence. We know them.

No matter what I considered accepting intellectually, I knew in my heart that now, as I faced the fear of losing Brio, I had to try my utmost to listen, to hear him as never before. I needed to know when it would be time to set him free and send him into that next gust of wind.

There is a wonderful term in Celtic mysticism—*mo anam cara.* *Anam* is the Gaelic word for "soul," and *cara* is the word for "friend," rendering "soul friend." The Irish poet, philosopher, and scholar John O'Donohue writes, "The *anam cara* was a person to whom you could reveal the hidden intimacies of your life. This friendship was an act of recognition and belonging. When you had an *anam cara,* your friendship cut across all convention and category. You were joined in an ancient and eternal way with the friend of your soul."[30]

I had my *anam cara.*

10

Days of the Hummingbird

The Hummingbird is a symbol of regeneration or resurrection. Hummingbird is the creature that opens the heart.[1]

TIME WAS FULL OF BRIO, FULL OF CARING FOR HIM, full of worrying, full of awe for his spirit, full of love. We'd moved to the country; his life was easier with no elevators, no concrete sidewalks. Carried outside, unable to walk on his own, Brio would lie in the grass to do his business. Then we'd move to a clean spot; he'd sniff the breeze. He'd lift his paw at me, wanting to show that he could play as we always did. I see him with his smile, eyes bright, speaking to me, telling me that he was there, always there. We shared many gazes in those days. He watched me move around the house; I watched him watching and wanted never to look away.

There was little sleep. He needed to be taken outdoors two or three times in the middle of the night. As the crickets whirred, as the stars shone or clouds passed over the moon, the moments stretched out, treasures to hold onto. There was magic in those days—how much I would soon come to realize.

The nights grew worse; he began to have some kind of seizures, probably heart-related the vet said. He would shake uncontrollably, his eyes glazed. All I could do was hold him until it passed. Tests and procedures were not recommended and made no sense at this point. One vet felt it was time to let go. Another, who knew him well and loved him, advised, "Not yet."

Even in the stress and the outward chaos, he was my anchor through it all. He came out of the seizures and slept and ate his breakfast and sniffed the breeze through the screen door. In our private moments, I whispered a mantra in his ear, "Never, ever leave me."

I wanted a pact. I said we would always give each other signs. Brio seemed to have an odd affinity for four-leaf clovers. I'd amassed a collection of them, because over the years Brio would often sit or lie down right next to one. It happened so frequently it seemed more than mere coincidence. I had come to see the clovers as confirmation that he had some special access to a mysterious realm from which he could manifest the clovers as gifts—as signs—to me. Part of me said, *You're crazy, that's only wishful thinking.* Another, more hopeful part, said, *It's true.*

I kept searching his eyes for guidance. I continued to feel him, to feel his spirit. *Not yet,* I thought. But in the evenings, doubt descended, and I called my animal communicators for guidance. I wanted them to confirm my own instincts. More than that, I wanted to know what they heard from Brio.

I didn't always get that. Often they sent me back into myself.

"Alecia, is he ready to go?" I asked with so much tightness in my voice that I could hardly utter the words.

The answer was about me, not Brio, and not really anything I didn't already know. "Two things are coming up," she said, "the fear of letting him go and the fear of letting him suffer. You have to separate what's rational and what's emotional. The rational part is 'I don't want this dog to suffer.' The emotional stuff is 'I don't know how I'm going to live without this dog and be okay.'"

I was growing afraid to leave him alone. Yet I desperately needed a short break. I planned to go up to Martha's Vineyard where we had gone together so many times. I told Alecia I thought the trip would be too much for Brio and that I would leave him for a few days with the woman who'd boarded him for many years. The answer was immediate, and seemingly direct from Brio. "He tells me, 'That doesn't feel right.' I'm asking him, 'What doesn't feel right?' It's almost like he has a knowing that he's going to go and for him it's like, 'No, we need to go out there and we need to have another great weekend and we need to spend this time together smiling, enjoying it.'"

Here was a message I didn't really want. I was ashamed of wanting to leave him behind and afraid, so afraid, that he would die in the car or on the island, away from home and help. I told myself, "Well, maybe this is Alecia talking, not Brio." But that didn't feel true.

Alecia—or Brio—didn't let up. "You think you really need a break. But he's insistent. 'I'm sorry but that's not what is going to happen.'" So we went. Alecia had said just to stay in the moment, to be always present. On the long six-hour car trip, I practiced that. I never lost the thought that he could go at any second, lying on the backseat. I clung to the conviction that this was what he wanted.

We made it, and his joy was palpable; I could see a spark, a light in his eyes as I lifted him in my arms to take him out of the car. His head was up. He was smelling the air. It was Vineyard grass and Vineyard smells and the sea breeze close, even that first night. At the beach, he even walked a bit with support to smell around the very rocks where he had always gone to check out recent dog visitors. We sat together on the rocks looking out to sea, and it felt like forever.

The second night he had a very bad attack. He lay gasping, eyes glassy, not seeing. As I sat through the dark hours holding him, feeling every labored breath, I thought this was probably it. At 4:00 a.m. I called Alecia in Colorado. It was 2:00 a.m. her time, and I woke her out of a sound sleep. She wasn't happy, but she agreed to connect with Brio and seemed to connect with him as quickly as ever. "He keeps saying, 'I'm not ready to go.' It's about you staying present without allowing your emotions to ricochet you."

The sun rose, and he still lay there, still with me. The local vet came and said it was not necessarily his time unless I decided it was. I could not. We had two more days at the ocean. On the last morning it was foggy and cool, with salt spray blowing in off the surf. I parked the car right at the edge of the bluff, by the rocks, looking out to the sea. I opened the side back door and sat with him, smelling his head as I always would when we sat together near the end of our beach walks, just looking out together. The wind blew his black curls. His head was up, looking straight ahead and far away, drinking in the wind and the sea smell and the light. It was blue-gray, ethereal, with just the hint of violet through the fog. After a long time, I got in the driver's seat and started the car down the road back to the cottage. But I could not leave yet. Back around I turned, back to our spot at the edge of the bluff. We needed more time, feeling the sea and this moment together.

I feel it now.

I knew how important this trip was. "As hard as it was at the time," I told Alecia, "I am so grateful we went."

"For him personally," she said, "he really wanted to be there because he wanted that last experience. He wanted to be out by the ocean. He really wanted to partake of it with you. But it was also part of his path to experience it before he left the planet; that freedom of being in a dog's body; the way you're able to experience things in a physical body. He wanted to feel the breeze running through his coat. The beauty that you went and you were in the present moment. It's so joyous."

We made the drive back home and settled into the days. He lay in the sun and ate well. I thought constantly of those last moments by the ocean, my head on his, smelling his curls, gazing out to the horizon.

A few weeks after we'd returned from Martha's Vineyard, Alecia suddenly echoed those very words that I'd been saying to Brio daily. "You've been saying, 'never, ever leave me,'" she whispered. I had never told her of the mantra. "Brio doesn't want to leave you," Alecia said, "but he can't stay in that body anymore. You need to tell him it's alright to go."

I had to be sure. "How do you know that?" I asked.

"He tells me," was the simple, confident answer.

The attacks initially had happened only at night. Now they began in the day. It became very difficult to leave him alone.

I also began to call Dawn several times a week, hoping—perhaps subconsciously—to hear someone contradict what Alecia was saying and my own instincts. She did not.

"It's getting harder," Dawn said. "His passing is close. It's his choice. His spiritual path is complete in this lifetime. His relationship with you is secure. He's done everything he needed to do."

I felt at last that it was indeed time—time to grant Brio the freedom to escape his suffering but also time to trust that the larger-than-life bond we'd developed would endure beyond death. It was time to test my faith in my newfound beliefs. I made arrangements for Brio's long-time vet from the city to come out in a few days, still grasping for hours, moments. And they did bring me treasures.

During those last days, I wasn't looking for Brio's four-leaf clovers—that sign between us. But one day as he lay in the grass I looked down and there was a four-leaf clover right in the middle of his flank, laid out for me as clear as could be!

I sat with him for hours on the kitchen floor. There we were again, his head collapsed on my lap just as it had been on that first day when I'd brought him home. Only now, unlike fifteen years ago, I couldn't imagine my life without—not my dog—my *soul mate*. Near the screen door, we could feel the summer breeze and hear the birds.

Other unusual things happened in those last days. Many will call them coincidences.

But I stopped believing in coincidences a long time ago.

Here in the country there were always animals around but never before had creatures come so close to the house or stayed so long. First, a frog appeared on the front path and just sat there for hours. Then a hummingbird hung endlessly right outside the screen door near where Brio and I sat. I had seen hummingbirds, but none had made a visitation like this and none ever did again while I was in that house. I felt somehow that they were there for Brio, to wish him on his way and accompany his journey.

The frog, because it's an amphibian that transforms itself, is considered a symbol of birth, death, and rebirth. In the High Andes of South America, the hummingbird is a symbol of resurrection because it seems lifeless at night in the cold and rebounds in the warmth of the sun. Hummingbirds are considered in many traditional cultures to be messengers between worlds. It's also thought that they carry powerful medicine, opening the heart to the happiness of life.[2]

Indeed, there was magic in those days.

Finally, one morning, I knew. The attacks were constant and devastating. I could not wait for my regular vet to come from New York City. The day was here. I arranged for a local vet to come that afternoon.

I had spent the night before lying next to him on his bed. He had breakfast, and we sat on that kitchen floor again. At lunchtime, I asked a friend to bring a pound of roast beef. We carried him outside and he lay in the grass, gobbling down the entire package. So Brio! Still, I knew it was time. Back inside, at our spot by the door, he gave a big sigh and laid his head on my chest. That was where he stayed; where he was when the vet arrived. I never let go of him.

I called Alecia. She'd arranged to be on the phone with me when the moment came. She stayed with me as I held Brio. I saw nothing, my head buried against his face. Brio was tranquillized, resting. I heard the vet ask if I was ready. Then I felt I was traveling with Brio. It was like being inside a centrifuge. I was whirling, whirling with him, going somewhere. For a moment it seemed I was being carried with him, borne by that energy. It was overwhelming, something I could not, would not, fight. I would have been alright going with him. In those moments there was no thought, no doubt, no pain, just sensation.

But then I felt he was off—I knew his energy was no longer in his body. For minutes I just sat there, still holding him.

"What was that?" I finally got out in a hoarse whisper. "Where is he?"

Evidently Alecia had somehow felt the same thing. "He was spinning. He was leaving his body. His energy came out of his body in a spiral stream returning to where it came from."

"What do you mean? Where is he?" I repeated. "Where did his energy go?" I could hardly absorb in that moment what Alecia then explained. "Look at it this way. If energy comes into the body in physical form and condenses itself, when it's leaving there's going to be a tremendous amount of expanse. It's like the amount of energy we have is so enormous and then it gets condensed down into little bodies. Then when it gets freed again it creates a huge vortex."

Animal communicator Margrit Coates has come to a similar conclusion based on her experience with animals as they pass over. "Energy cannot be destroyed, only converted from one form to another. As all living beings are energy forms, this is a property of energy that they too must surely obey. This means a soul that has left the Earth plane, whilst invisible to us, is not lost to us. . . . On countless occasions when I have been present at an animal's physical death, I have felt a surge of energy in my hands, a tapping or spiraling sensation under my palms, or a subtle change in the surrounding atmosphere if I have not actually been touching the animal."[3]

"I just remember how enormous his energy was," Alecia continued. "It's like you took a star and it just exploded through the universe. That's what I mean by the difference between the physical energy and the energy of the full consciousness of the being once it's out of the body. I was blown away by how enormous and how loving it was."

I know the truth of what I felt. And it was echoed in Alecia's words. The sensation of that vortex was not something I thought or imagined. It was physical. I felt it. I experienced it. It had nothing to do with my own shock and grief. When it was over, when Brio had passed, I was in shock but I had no physical aftereffects such as dizziness or lightheadedness. It was Brio's energy that had carried me into the spiral. I felt he had taken me part of the way with him—perhaps one more lesson he came into my life to teach me.

I now knew that neither he nor I were limited to our physical bodies. There is a consciousness, an individual consciousness, that I completely felt even as I spun around and out—out of my physical body. I see that lesson now with clarity, though at the time the experience was too overwhelming to fully absorb. I see too that in my life before Brio I had avoided difficult emotional situations; avoided feeling too much. Yet there was never a moment's hesitation in my decision to be with Brio through his passage, the most difficult situation of all.

Dawn Hayman gave me a gift. She counsels many a dog person before and after their companion's passing. But it seemed, as she spoke with me day after day before Brio physically died, that she too had felt something special going on.

"This is where it became really, really clear that your relationship with Brio was different from what most people have," Dawn explained. "You allowed him to go through his process very consciously. He died exactly as he wanted to go. That's not as common for animals as it should be. A lot of people euthanize early because feelings are coming up and they get scared and say, 'I can't deal with that.' It's easier to euthanize. What you did that's different is that you really stayed totally present with him. He wanted to share this with you like he shared the rest of his life. That's what he came into this life to do, to experience a relationship like that with you. There's no bigger thing than to go through a relationship like that and say it's complete and whole. It's beautiful to watch. As hard as it is to hear what he had to say, you were open to hearing him. I'm not sure you understood it as you did it, but you allowed yourself to go through it. And you allowed him to take you on the journey he took you on."

From that moment there was no turning back. I had, for a moment, touched the other world, that "other side" so often feared and revered yet scarcely comprehensible. I now felt an overwhelming need to know as much as possible about the truth of the afterlife. I believed, more than ever, that consciousness may survive physical death.

11

Out of Thin Air

THE NIGHT AFTER BRIO'S PASSING, all the lights in the house went out. There was a storm, but no general power outage in the area. The fuses just blew inexplicably. One of my friends who had gathered to give support said it was Brio showing he was still around. Why not believe it? Why not believe that somehow he continued to exist, since it was impossible to think that he had suddenly ceased to exist? Why not consider that the huge energy of his spirit was continuing to affect the material world? I was coming to the resounding realization that being a believer was bringing color into my world—a black-and-white world that had long been drained by disbelief and negativity. At night, as I lay between wakefulness and sleep, I could feel him. I often had lain on his flank, feeling his heartbeat, his breathing. Now it truly seemed that I could still feel his presence, the life of his spirit.

I had recently begun to explore different spiritual paths, going to some group classes in Siddha yoga and reading the teachings of a mystic Catholic priest whom I filmed. Everything felt like very foreign territory to me still, but some of it resonated deeply, like a truth I had always known but had chosen to forget. I began to meditate from time to time. In the beginning, thoughts and fears crowded my mind. Yes, I read that that was normal. But like most new meditators, I was convinced I was doing it wrong. I took periods off, but kept coming back.

I'd gotten enough of a glimpse of what inner stillness meant as I sat with Brio in a flower shop or at the ocean just breathing that salt air that filled me with joy and hope. I continued to try to find that stillness within myself. I don't remember exactly when it happened, but the time I first truly "felt" and even "saw" Brio in meditation, after he had physically died, is forever ingrained in my mind. At first it was more a feeling, a sense of his presence. Then his face arose in my mind's eye, so clearly that I could discern different expressions or movements of his head. It was so clearly *him*—the way he held his head, the starry gaze. In meditation, there was a knowing, an absolute knowing that I had seen him in spirit, although my rational mind still couldn't explain this experience. I hung on to every millisecond of these feelings and moments of conviction that he was still with me.

Was Brio in fact still with me somehow? Would he come back physically? The mere thought of seeing him again in flesh and blood made me feel that I could come home again, that I could feel again that I belonged.

Perhaps it wouldn't happen quite like that, but Brio and I were ever-connected in a way that was just as "real" as physical life. Indeed, I had stepped further into the world of Spirit in the last days of Brio's physical presence. That day before he passed, when the hummingbird and the frog appeared, I felt I was living between two worlds. I was there on the kitchen floor holding Brio, but I somehow knew that these appearances of the frog and the hummingbird were truly from the world of Spirit. People could argue that they were just coincidence, but in my heart, in the part of me that was now awakened to another dimension, I knew they belonged to that other plane of reality. They had invited me in.

In the days after Brio passed, this other dimension of Spirit was more real to me than the ordinary physical world. I sleepwalked through the daily tasks of "normal reality." I surely was not wholly there. My need to know that Brio still existed in some way was all-consuming. I was driven to seek affirmation of the continuance of life, of the unbroken bond.

In the soft space of the summer nights, when he was no longer visible physically, it was easy to let my imagination travel, to feel him just beyond the reach of touch and sight. He was everywhere: looking at me as I got ready for sleep as he always had, or lying on his bed in the sun, or on the grass under the moonlight. Those were the good moments, when I felt his presence, felt the conviction of it. Yet often I seemed to be reaching in vain past the horizon line. When Brio had gazed so intently out over the ocean, I always felt he could see beyond it. So why couldn't I?

Surely the next step into nonphysical dimensions was not a matter to be explained or discussed. I could not explain it to myself. If I had been in the shallows of psychic phenomenon, I now plunged into the surf. I wanted to hear from Brio, from the world of Spirit. I wanted to see what the communicators would "report" about Brio and if it felt true or not.

I asked Dawn to try to connect with him. There was something about her "down-to-earthness," her funny, rather blunt manner that I wanted; something I felt might give assurance that I hadn't gone completely crazy in trying to believe in a reality of existence beyond what our physical senses can know. I told Dawn nothing of the last days with Brio, nothing of my experience during those moments of his passing when I'd been on the phone with Alecia.

"I sat under a little tree and ate roast beef," were the first words out of Dawn's mouth. "He enjoyed the moment," she went on. "He wants you to feel him there in that spot." I'd said nothing about how I had in fact sat with Brio in the yard and fed him an entire pound of roast beef.

After the years of uncannily accurate readings when Brio was physically here, I shouldn't have been completely surprised that somehow Dawn was still apparently hearing him so accurately. Still, it took my breath away.

"He wants you to feel him in connection with your heart, to feel his love for you; he feels it." Dawn's words were, of course, what I wanted to hear, wanted to believe in. But how could she have known?

How could I not feel that she was truly somehow hearing Brio's voice?

The devil's advocate in me argued that she could be reading *my* mind. Even if it was too much to believe that she was just guessing, giving a cold reading, there could be some other explanation. Maybe it was not just a matter of "hearing" Brio. Maybe she was somehow tapping into a dimension where there was no time or space. But such mental excursions into unfathomable territory gave me no comfort. Again, I was insatiable in my quest for confirmation that Brio's presence was still here; that what one animal communicator said could be verified by another.

I asked Alecia, "Where is he?"

But Alecia pushed back. "I don't really like to connect with them for the first three days at least. I want to let them be and go on their way, because we're so caught up in the physical strings. We have to be fair to him so he can complete his turnover."

"Why three days?" I wondered.

"I don't remember where I read it or heard it," Alecia explained, "but I felt something about how after passing there's a three-day ascension process."

Three days later Alecia checked back in with me to give me her report. "After passing he seems well. He's more solidified and oriented, running and playing. He's more like a puppy—the energy around him. That dog was an amazing runner with these super-duper long strides. And he showed me a vision of him just running and playing and having fun. I've had that a number of times with dogs that lose bodily functions. When they transition they say look, 'Look, I'm out of my physical body. Look at what I can do! I'm free now.'"

Remember that Alecia had only been in Brio's actual physical presence once—she never saw him running, never observed him outside of my home.

I went back to the ocean on Martha's Vineyard—my first visit without Brio, the first in fifteen years. The days there seemed to be out of a dream; a time not of this world. In meditation I felt Brio's presence.

I could feel him in the wind, as I lay in the grass where he had rolled with joy, legs kicking the air. The doubting part of me argued that this could be just wishful thinking or a product of my subconscious, even though there was an internal knowing that it was more than that. That knowing part of me was gaining strength, almost enough to shut down the skeptical part.

After I returned home, I again called Dawn, wondering what she might "hear" from Brio, if he had truly been with me on the island when I felt his presence in an especially powerful way. I told Dawn nothing about the visit, yet she said right away, "You went to the ocean with his ashes. Brio was walking with you on the beach."

I had scattered some of his ashes there on the rocks edging the sand and into the ocean as well. He would want, I knew, to be part of the ocean that he'd loved. It was hard, so hard, to hold that gray dust in my hand and believe that that was Brio. In fact, as much as I yearned for his physical body, I did know that he was not really in those ashes. They did not hold his great energy. So I could believe that he had in some sense been walking with me—in spirit—on the beach. I had seen paw prints in the sand and wondered if somehow they were Brio's. But Dawn didn't confirm that bit of magical thinking. "The paw prints were not his. But he says you sat on a little grassy knoll near the edge of the water. He knows you can feel him in your heart. Brio wants you to know he's still here." She meant, of course, that his essence, his presence, was with me.

I had, in fact, sat on some rocks elevated above the beach; there were grassy green dunes right behind me.

I found it more convincing that when it came to the paw prints, Dawn drew a clear distinction between my desire to believe and what she felt was actually true about Brio's presence with me that day on the beach. The fact that she didn't just confirm everything I wanted to believe led me to trust her more and to think that perhaps—just perhaps—there is a reality in which Brio exists, in which he sits with me at the edge of the ocean.

But were my regular go-to communicators getting it right because they were already well aware of my history with Brio? Would someone new to the scene be able to contact him?

For the first time, I reached out to a different kind of psychic. Silvia Rossi, who calls herself a psychic medium, can apparently communicate with people—with beings—both before and after their physical death. She says she's had that ability since she was a child. Like other psychics, Silvia was initially surprised and mystified. She describes "inexplicable communications from the spirit side," seeing "shadows" and "people" at the foot of her bed. She resisted these experiences for many years until she came to appreciate and use what she now sees as her "gift." She's worked with the police to solve cold cases and murder cases. She's counseled families of 9/11 victims. Silvia is a Cuban American born in Miami and now a Jersey girl who loves to sing.

All of the animal communicators I know claim that they can continue to make contact after physical death. They argue that the energy of a being—human or animal—remains reachable in some way, because that energy never dies; it is only transferred from vessel to vessel.

But mediumship? I'd always cringed at anything that smacked of what became known in the 1970s as the New Age culture. It still seemed cultish to me, an outgrowth of the hippie movement, which could not be further from what I considered my natural inclinations.

The history of mediumship of course begins much earlier. Throughout human history there have been efforts to communicate with the dead. During the nineteenth century, mediumship gained popularity in the United States and in the United Kingdom, although along with this were widespread accounts of fraud. Critics pointed out that some mediums (like some psychics) did so-called cold readings, using peoples' dress or body language or response to leading questions to make educated guesses. Mediums especially, it was argued, preyed on grief. Yet interest in contacting the spirit world does not seem to have waned. Roper polls conducted over the years from 1944 to 2014 reported that the number of Americans believing in life after death has remained at about 7 in every 10 people since the 1960s. And the surveys reported that only about half of Americans rule out entirely the possibility that some people can communicate with the dead.[1] A professor who led a 1993 study at the University of California, Santa Barbara said, "People today are on a quest rather than in search of faith. They are walking, exploring, experimenting; they want to know the options. The quest itself has become in a sense a religious style."[2]

In short, I was not alone. Just as with the pet psychics many years ago, I was willing to experiment. There was no feeling of "woo-woo" at all in Silvia Rossi's tone, which gave me confidence. One would never think that she "talks to dead people," as she puts it. Silvia had never met Brio when he was alive, and I told her nothing about him when we first spoke by phone. Yet from the beginning her readings made it impossible not to believe that she was truly connected to Brio.

With no prompting, Silvia too picked up on my time after Brio's passing, when I'd been back at the ocean. "Brio is on the beach. He walked a lot; he walked with you on the sand, giving you signs. He knows that you talked to him a lot. You said, 'Brio, please give me signs. Brio, I miss you; please come back.' He says you got something to eat at the beach. He was there. You brought something to read."

Letter perfect! It's all in the details. How could she possibly have known what I said to Brio mentally, and that I'd brought a snack and a book to the beach. The details made me feel that those times when I imagined—actually *felt*—Brio beside me at the beach or walking with me or in the kitchen eating from his dish that I couldn't bear to remove, that those moments were valid even if invisible.

Silvia continued on to a lunch I'd had with a friend that same day. "There was someone who smoked. The smell of smoke bothered him." Actually, there had been a smoky fire in a fireplace, which filled the restaurant with smoke. That incident had been the last thing on my mind when I was speaking with Silvia. I'd forgotten all about it. Again, this kind of very particular detail, seemingly pulled out of thin air, made it seem so true that Brio must have been with me at that meal. The more clues like this that I got, the more I gained confidence in my own inner sense that the bond with Brio was still there. I tried to encourage that confidence. I called out to Brio in my mind, and sometimes out loud when I was alone, asking him to give me a sign of his presence.

In the past, I had had a couple of rare moments when I spontaneously felt such a strong connection to someone—someone still alive but nowhere near me in physical space—that I had no doubt there was some other reality in which we were together. Space was not a boundary blocking our connection. I thought of that moment as Brio was leaving this world, when I moved toward believing that there *can* be communication past death, past time as well as space.

Now that I'd stepped into this strange world I kept playing devil's advocate, asking myself if what I was hearing could be explained in some way that fit with the rational, material world of our five senses and that can be empirically tested by science. But oh, the details I was hearing!

Quite frequently, Silvia would report that Brio was in various places in my house that she had neither seen in person nor in photographs, nor had I described them to her. In one conversation, she reported: "He spends time in the bedroom. There's a light headboard with a pretty pattern." Yes, there was. I thought of the many times Brio had physically lain in his bed beside mine, or on my bed itself, right next to that headboard. That brought me comfort, thinking that perhaps he was remembering that too, and that perhaps he was even somehow looking at that headboard as Silvia spoke to me.

Another time, I called Silvia from my office at my house in the country. "There's a chair where you are now. It has wheels," she said. "I see Brio with you now. There's a door to the right. He's looking in the door. There's pretty trim at the bottom of the wall and a wood floor. There's a window opposite up against the corner. He's standing there in the doorway, saying, 'I'm here.'" As she was speaking, I looked at the door to my right, almost convinced that I would see Brio standing on the wood floor.

She went on to describe the dining room with equal accuracy. "There's a yellow color, or butter cream." Brio used to lie quite often in the dining room, which was painted a pale yellow cream color. There were chairs with a floral pattern. By now, I was incredulous. Sure, I wanted to believe. And the accuracy practically forced me to believe that Silvia was somehow seeing through Brio's eyes, right in my dining room.

"You've never seen my house. I've never described it to you," I told Silvia. "How can you possibly know these details? How can Brio somehow be 'telling' you this? Is he in this room; in the office with me right now?" I was clenching the phone, trying to hold on to material reality.

"Brio is not in a physical body," Sylvia answered, "but he'll come in free form to say 'hello.' He can be in constant communication and you may not feel him or sense him, even though you're thinking about him a lot and saying, 'Oh Brio, I miss you,' when in fact he's right there with you."

It was like explaining advanced physics to a two-year-old. The psychics had no way to give me an intellectually convincing argument. But I didn't feel that they were trying to defraud me and just take my money.

Sometimes Silvia and the animal psychics seemed to be exercising a kind of remote viewing. The term refers to the ability of some people to actually put themselves in a distant place and describe it. Scientific studies have not validated these claims, although the U.S. federal government actually invested in research into it during the 1990s. Stephan Schwartz, a former assistant to the chief of naval operations, is a leading expert on distant or remote viewing. He's conducted various experiments testing the ability of people with apparent remote-viewing ability to locate lost archaeological sites, sunken ships, or other distant objects whose whereabouts were unknown. Schwartz says that these individuals were able to accomplish these tasks, providing solid proof of distant viewing. The experiments were filmed and shown on national television.[3] Schwartz believes that remote viewing is evidence of what he calls non-local consciousness, which extends beyond our five physical senses and is not limited by time and space.

Mainstream science has not accepted remote viewing as a proven fact. However, it is a fact that the U.S. government invested research funds to investigate its possibilities. Ingo Swann was a renowned remote viewer in the twentieth century. He helped develop a process for experiments at the Stanford Research Institute in which viewers would try to "see" a location with no information except its geographical coordinates.[4] The process was tested with CIA funding during the 1970s.[5]

What about some of the "farther-out" theories regarding the possibility of continued existence or consciousness after physical death? I wondered, if matter and energy are interchangeable as physics tells us, does that mean that Brio's energy didn't die but continues to exist in some other form? Albert Einstein himself did not believe in the afterlife, although he was a mystic. He did state that "people like us, who believe in physics, know that the distinction between past, present, and future is only a stubbornly persistent illusion." So if individual consciousness, or awareness, of a being exists now in this moment, might it not exist in what we perceive as the future too?[6]

"Everything lives," Alecia Evans responded to my speculation. "Everything has essence to them that physical death doesn't conquer. Physical death just releases that energy to the universe. We struggle with loss as human beings. It's a hard thing to try to bridge the gap."

Throughout human history, many cultures have honored all creatures as equal to humans and even as having special power to help us from the spirit world—a perspective that often seems forgotten in the modern world. Native Americans have long believed that we all have animal spirits that help us through life. They honor them in ritual practices intended to help connect people to these animal totems, which are seen as supernatural guides who offer their power to human beings.[7]

The ancient practice of shamanism dates back at least 40,000 years ago, according to archaeological evidence, and perhaps to 100,000 years.[8] It's been practiced in many parts of the world, including Siberia,

Asia, Europe, Africa, and North and South America. Shamanism teaches that everything is alive and holds power—human beings, other creatures, plants, trees, rocks, the elements. Shamans believe—like Native Americans—that we all have power or spirit animals who act like guardian angels.[9]

Sandra Ingerman has been practicing and writing about shamanism since 1980. She explains that "a shaman is a man or woman who uses the ability to see 'with the strong eye'. . . . A shaman interacts directly with the spirits." She says that shamanism is a "system of direct revelation"—that is, the shaman communicates directly with the spirits, be they human spirits or power animals.[10]

Diana Leslie is a spiritual teacher in Connecticut who trained in shamanism ten years ago. She does not practice as a shaman today but incorporates it into her teaching. "It's not a religion in the sense that it doesn't have a specific set of beliefs or tenets," she told me. "It has generalized form. What it says is that you can communicate with anything. I like to believe that thousands of years ago humans were in much closer contact with the consciousness of everything else on the earth and maybe in the stars. As humans developed to be more materially oriented . . . I think that meant we lost some of that capacity. We lost our knowledge of how to really see all the other creatures as allies, rather than something that evolved into something we could dominate."

Leslie has had several power animals—a bear, a raven, a hummingbird among others. She's also had very close connections with animals she's shared her life with. So for her, there are connections to animals in two senses—to the totem or power animals who are guides, and also to those with whom she bonded in the physical world. "I've had conversations with ministers," she recalls, "who say of course animals don't have souls. I just can't believe that."

Leslie remarks: "It's not surprising to me that there is now interest in this whole notion of consciousness and being in connection with the animals and other spirit helpers. When I say *consciousness* I would say that's the equivalent of having a soul, that everything is connected and part of the Divine. You could call it 'Spirit '. . . or higher consciousness. But we're all connected."

Leslie sees signs now that there's a desire to receive knowledge of our ancestors that was lost along the way. "I'd like to think that doorways are opening." She herself has found it has been a long process to step away from the world of reason and empirical evidence and learn to trust a deeper knowledge within. There it was again—an echo of what the communicators had told me about their self-doubt when they first began to "hear" animals.

Brio, of course, was not a totem or emblem, not a spirit animal in that sense, for he was alive in a physical form. But, regardless, his soul was deeply entwined with mine, and in that regard I certainly considered him my spirit animal. This was reinforced when Leslie said to me, "I could posit that your soul is using the dog to communicate. I consider that to be a channel of information."

The psychics had gone a long way in making the endurance of Spirit authentic to me, not to mention consoling me in a time of great need. They'd given a lot of details that seemed to be accurate communication from Brio about his experiences just before and after his physical death.

And yet my rational mind continued to seek answers to how exactly the psychics could still be getting messages from Brio. If we grant that an individual spirit does endure, how could it communicate with those still physically alive? A dog had led me to ask these biggest questions of all. I was coming to a point at which I no longer expected an answer in human, material terms. I was out there now in the world of metaphysics—beyond the physical. And this strange territory continued to surprise me and pull me further into the quest to know more.

12

To Reincarnate or Not to Reincarnate

THERE WAS NO DENYING THE ACCURACY OF INFORMATION apparently coming from Brio in spirit through our translators; I could not help but feel that his spirit continued to exist, that our bond was unbroken. Still, there was the yearning for his physical return. As I began to search for a puppy who would be "Brio-returned," I also delved into philosophical, religious/spiritual, and scientific thought about reincarnation.

I had believed in reincarnation as a child. It was almost a knowing, as I recall. I once had a sense of a place and culture where I'd been many centuries ago, though no recollection of past lives. I just recall a frisson of recognition as I was reading a history book and came across a passage about Chichén Itzá, the pre-Columbian city built by the Mayans in what is now the Mexican Yucatán. Filled with excitement and an absolute conviction, I ran to tell my mother and grandmother. My revelation that I'd thought so thrilling was instantly poo-pooed as "just your imagination." As I've since learned, that's a common reaction by parents in the Western world when hearing their children express a belief in reincarnation.

Put it down to childhood imagination if you will, but that moment of discovery—and even realization—became embedded in my memory.

It had never left me, even though I learned not to speak of that childhood conviction and came to view it myself as possibly just a flight of fancy and something that didn't quite fit with the world of fact and reason—certainly not with the journalistic requirement of hard evidence. Then Brio's physical death propelled me toward a new exploration of the idea of physical afterlife. Could Brio really come back?

My subconscious fear of losing my dog was playing out in my dreams. I had recurring dreams of losing Brio. I would search for him—searching and searching—because without him I felt lost. But perhaps my sleeping visions hinted at a different truth: that our current connection had been inspired long, long ago. That I, perhaps, had known Brio in former lives. That Brio and I had lost and found each other over and over again—in different times, circumstances, and disguises.

Now I searched again. I remembered what my friend had said about Brio: "You can see the pyramids in his eyes." I now sought to discover the many lives of Brio that had so changed mine. I recalled the ayurvedic doctor who said he was an old soul. I recalled the chiropractor David Mehler's statement that Brio had been "some sort of a king in a different lifetime."

Skepticism about any belief in an afterlife and reincarnation has ruled in the West ever since the Age of Enlightenment, centered in the eighteenth century, promoted the rationalist philosophy of the French philosopher René Descartes. The Age of Reason and the scientific revolution were close relations.[1]

So perhaps it comes as a surprise to many people—as it did to me, frankly—that the West nevertheless inherited, from Greek philosophy, a quite different thread of historical belief regarding reincarnation. Pythagoras was famous for his mathematical theories—particularly in relation to the foundations of music. But in his time he was also known for his teachings of a doctrine called metempsychosis, which held that the soul doesn't die and undergoes a cycle of rebirths. Another fascinating thing: Pythagoras apparently believed that the soul of a human could be reborn in the body of an animal. And the story goes that, in the howl of a dog, he believed he'd heard the voice of a friend who'd died.[2]

Plato also believed in metempsychosis—reincarnation. He thought a fixed number of souls existed. Therefore they had to keep returning in different bodies. He wrote, "That is the conclusion, I said; and if a true conclusion, then the souls must always be the same, for if none be destroyed they will not diminish in number."[3]

The ideas of these Greeks about an afterlife and reincarnation seem strikingly similar to the beliefs of Eastern religions, which hold that our souls reincarnate until we've reached enlightenment. Buddhist scholar and the author of this book's foreword, Robert Thurman, points out that it's believed that the Buddha himself had reincarnations as animals. He spoke of it himself, Thurman explains. "He was a lion. He was a frog, and other animals. Buddhists believe that humans have been animals and animals can be reborn as humans."

I remembered what the ayurvedic healer had said—that Brio wouldn't come back as a dog. Can animals reincarnate as humans?

The West, though remaining largely skeptical, has come to accept the notion of reincarnation to some degree. Indeed, as recent interest continues to develop in the field of spirituality, there is a deepening curiosity about the "transmigration of souls," as Pythagoras put it.

The notion that souls not only live on but come back has drawn serious attention from a few researchers. The most notable is the late Dr. Ian Stevenson, founder and director of the Division of Perceptual Studies at the University of Virginia. Stevenson traveled the world for forty years, investigating thousands of cases of children who claimed to remember past lives. He documented physical and psychological qualities in many of these children that resembled people who had died.

Stevenson's work was widely criticized. Yet the work of the Division of Perceptual Studies continues under the leadership of Jim Tucker, a professor of psychiatry and neurobehavioral sciences. He focuses on American cases in his research at the Virginia Foundation. "Over the decades," Tucker told me, "we've now studied over twenty-five hundred cases of children who report memories of past lives."

One of the most publicized was that of a young boy who remembered in detail the life of a World War II pilot killed in a crash. James Leininger, born in Louisiana, was around two years old when he started having constant nightmares of being in a plane crash. He said he'd been a pilot in World War II and had flown off a boat when he was shot down. He recalled the name of the boat and the name of a friend and colleague—a fellow crew member who was also killed. Research proved that there was in fact an aircraft carrier with the name James had given. A plane had indeed crashed as James described, and the pilot in the plane next to his bore the name James had said was that of his friend.[4]

I asked Tucker if he'd ever encountered reincarnation stories involving animals—people remembering lives as animals. He said he had not. But he told me Ian Stevenson had alluded to some such cases in his book *Children Who Remember Previous Lives*. Stevenson wrote, "After I overcame an initial prejudice against such cases, I conscientiously recorded notes of whatever anyone wished to tell me about them, and yet I have notes about fewer than thirty cases of claimed nonhuman animal rebirth altogether. Most of them have as their subject a human who has said that he had an incarnation as a nonhuman animal. Sometimes such an animal life occurred as an 'intermediate' life between another human life and the subject's present one."

But how can there be proof of a past life as an animal—of an animal reincarnating then as a human? Stevenson added, "The cases of claimed lives as nonhuman animals can, in the nature of things, offer little evidence of the kind that we have found in the ordinary human cases, and most of them provide no evidence whatever—merely the subject's unsupported claim that he had such an incarnation."[5]

Jim Tucker agrees that "it's difficult to map these cases onto a materialist understanding of reality . . . if the physical world is all there is, then I don't know how you can accept these cases and believe in them. But I think there are good reasons to think that consciousness can be considered a separate entity from physical reality." Tucker continues, "I think these cases contribute to the body of evidence that consciousness . . . can survive the death of the body; that life after death isn't necessarily just a fantasy or something to be considered on faith, but it can also be approached in an analytic way, and the idea can be judged on its merits."[6]

Tucker points to quantum physics, which proposes that physical "reality" is actually shaped by the observer, that consciousness is creating the material world. Max Planck, the founder of quantum theory said, "I regard consciousness as fundamental. I regard matter as derivative from consciousness."[7] So, Tucker argues, "in that case, it would mean that consciousness would not necessarily be dependent on a physical brain in order to survive, and it could continue to survive . . . after the body dies." Tucker believes that individual consciousness may continue after death and return in a future life.[8]

There are other physicists who have come forward in recent years to propose that quantum theory supports the idea of an afterlife and even reincarnation.[9] For example, the late Dr. Hans-Peter Durr, former head of the Max Planck Institute for Physics in Munich, cited the wave-particle dualism of atomic particles (the concept that they can exist as both wave and particle) stating that it applies to everything in the universe living and dead—a quantum code.

Therefore, Dr. Durr told an interviewer, "I imagine that I have written my existence in this world on a sort of hard drive on the tangible (the brain), that I have also transferred this data onto the spiritual quantum field, then I could say that when I die, I do not lose this information, this consciousness. The body dies but the spiritual quantum field continues. In this way, I am immortal."[10]

Rupert Sheldrake, the Cambridge University–trained biologist, approaches the questions of afterlife and reincarnation from the point of view of his own theory of "morphic fields." He theorizes that living beings are linked and communicate through these fields and proposes that this invisible field may endure after physical death.

Sheldrake is often asked how his theory shapes his ideas on the existence of soul and of whether the soul survives physical death. He has said that the theory of morphic fields is akin to the ideas of Aristotle and St. Thomas Aquinas, who thought of soul not as a spiritual concept but as part of nature, that which organizes living bodies.

"In that sense," Sheldrake says, "all morphic fields of plants and animals are like souls. The theory I'm putting forth," he explains, "is one that would see the soul normally associated with the body and memories coming about by morphic resonance. If a soul in that sense survives the death of the body there could be a continuation of consciousness." But Sheldrake cautions that there's nothing in his theory of morphic fields that proves the survival of the soul in any sense of the word; but neither does it disprove it. He does pose an interesting theory that if memories of other beings exist in a morphic field, then perhaps the living could tap into those memories without actually being the reincarnation of those who have passed.[11] "The idea that there could be a disembodied morphic field is going way beyond my normal hypothesis," he told me, "but I'm open to considering it."

The research is fascinating for would-be believers. For skeptics, it means little. The debate has often simply come down to a war between two worldviews, one wedded to the materialist concept of reality defined by the five senses, the other open to exploring the intangible and ineffable.

What seems to be different now is that more scientists are stepping into that mysterious territory. The theories of scientists such as Rupert Sheldrake and quantum physicists are fascinating and compelling. For a layperson, however, they remain remote, beyond the reach of deep understanding. Thus, for me and others who seek support when entertaining a belief in the possible reincarnation of a beloved animal, the emotional and intuitive sustenance for such belief comes from personal testimony.

Needless to say, there's no research like Ian Stevenson and Jim Tucker's studies with humans about the possible afterlife and reincarnation of other species. These other creatures can't tell us about past lives—certainly not in human language. So people like me turn to psychics and intuitives for guidance.

The animal communicators I've met do believe in the possibility that dogs, like people, can reincarnate. They tell stories of animals, dogs and horses, who "told" them of past lives. Some believe they themselves have had animals who have come back, and they cite clients who are sure beloved companions have physically come back to them.

Nancy Kaiser, a communicator based in North Carolina, strongly believes that many of her own animals have returned in other forms—a horse, for example, returning as a kitten on a client's farm.[12] It's predictable that animal communicators would personally hold such beliefs. So I find that often the stories of their clients—"ordinary" people who've come to think, to their surprise, that reincarnation has actually happened with their animals—are especially intriguing.

One of Nancy Kaiser's clients, a former highly successful marketing executive in Massachusetts, told me one such fascinating tale. "It's a love story," Barbara Barber said right away—"a fabulous love story." Barber had had thirteen dogs throughout her life but had always wanted a chocolate lab. Some years ago, the right puppy finally came along and she got Cocoa, who became adored by Barbara, her husband, and their twins. "She was an absolutely wonderful puppy. She was the best dog on the planet."

But when Cocoa was only four years old, she became ill with cancer and passed away. "It was devastating; it was just unbelievable," Barber says. Desperate for a dog, she soon got a rescue dog. But he had major temperament issues and sadly had to be put down because he was biting children.

On the day Barber went to the vet's office to pick up the dog's ashes, she saw—right by the door as she entered—a chocolate lab puppy, a female. "The dog looked at me and I looked at the dog and I just melted. That dog and I just fell in love. She went nuts," Barber recalls. As she left, Barber said to the owner of the puppy that if she ever found she could not keep the dog, Barber would take her.

Thinking that the owner probably thought she was crazy, Barber thought no more of it, but then she got a call from the vet's office saying the puppy's owner wanted to get in touch with her. They became friends, meeting a few times with the puppy, who, incidentally, had been named Cocoa by her owner! About two months later the puppy owner called and said she had a new boyfriend and new job. Cocoa was alone all day. Could Barber take her? "Absolutely," was the answer, and Barber picked up Cocoa number 2 that evening.

When she got the puppy home, "everything was so familiar," Barber says. Cocoa number 1 had often slept on the second stair from the top. Cocoa number 2 picked the same spot. When Barber's now ex-husband visited the house and Cocoa saw him for the first time it seemed like instant recognition. "No one can tell me different," Barber stresses. "I've had thirteen dogs, and this was instant recognition. No question."

Barber is not religious. She is spiritual, she says, but "Whether I'm spiritual or not there is no question in my mind that this dog came to me on purpose to help me through a very rough time in my life." I wondered if Barber had ever imagined that one of her dogs would reincarnate and come back to her. "I had never given it a thought that an animal might come back," she told me, "I'd never given it a thought."

Communicator Cindy Brody admits that when she first began "talking" to animals she had doubts about reincarnation. "I thought, 'Well, maybe that's just wishful thinking, being hopeful,'" she told me. But now, after years of experience, she too is convinced that some animals return physically.

People who are convinced that their animals have returned to them in other bodies often cite behavior that seems to mimic that of the animal who has passed. Barbara Barber's "recognition" of Cocoa number 2 as Cocoa seemed to her to be confirmed by the dog's behavior, which echoed the behavior of Cocoa number 1.

Whatever one finds in these stories, there is no question that they are about hope—about people faced with apparent endings who see continuation and connection. Lisa L., a dog lover in New Jersey, has loved and lost (at least initially) several dogs. Eight years ago, the terminal illness of one of her golden retrievers named Rose and her adoption of another drove her to consult an animal communicator. She has never looked back; she's now a firm believer that Rose has come back to her as her new dog. She's also found that her dialogue with a communicator, her translator, has changed her relationship with all her dogs.

"It's an amazing experience," Lisa told me, "to have someone who can communicate with your animals and help you when you don't know what's going on and also just to get to know them better. I said to her one day that the neatest thing is getting to know what your dog's real personality is like. It has helped me cope with a lot of things that have happened . . . even losing other dogs. It's very comforting for me to know that they're around me."

Nancy Kaiser speaks of how her work communicating with animals has changed her: "Talking with animals that have died taught me that death wasn't the big final Nothing that most people fear. . . . I prefer the term *transition,* which better describes what actually happens. Transition/death is nothing more than a change in form. The energy that comprises our soul vibrates very slowly while in the physical body. When the body dies and the soul is released, the energy returns to a rapidly vibrating spiritual state."[13]

Actually, the more I sought Brio's physical return, the more I *felt* his presence. Unlike some people who hear barks in the night or feel the tapping of paws after their dog has passed, I couldn't see Brio's presence, or hear it, or smell it. But the feeling of it was solidly within me. Sometimes I could truly sense him walking beside me. I've come to think that perhaps we humans may have too narrow a definition of existence. Cindy Brody believes our fellow animals can teach us a different perspective. "We cling to life too much," Brody told me. "Between life and death is just a thin line. Animals know that. When we, or they, lose physical being, we become energy, consciousness."

It was Einstein, of course, who taught us that energy and matter are interchangeable, that energy never dies. So if we think of consciousness or soul as energy can we not imagine that perhaps it's possible for that energy to go out into the beyond—just as I felt Brio's spirit spiraling outward to take on new form?

Dawn had explained her view this way: "The soul is too big for one body. The lifetime of Brio is just one fingerprint. It comes back with another form, another unique fingerprint." As to if and when he would reincarnate, she continued, "The energy of the soul goes back into a body." So, yes, maybe that new form would be in spirit. But in the first months after Brio passed, I just wanted Brio back as a dog! I could not accept having him only in spirit. So the frantic search for a puppy who would embody Brio's next life began. I researched breeders and sought some sign, some feeling that I was being led to the puppy who would be Brio. Of course I kept asking the communicators if I was on the right track.

I did not always hear what I wanted to hear. Some of the animal psychics did not think Brio would return—at least not now. In fact, the majority felt "no," he would not. I looked for additional opinions. I phoned Donna Lozito, a communicator in Arizona who had been recommended by a friend. The friend had told her nothing about Brio or me. Donna gained my trust early on by picking up on Brio's breed, physical troubles, and character. But she didn't hesitate to disappoint either, by saying she doubted Brio would reincarnate, at least not then.

Margrit Coates, the well-known animal communicator in England, believes that "animals have a choice as to whether they wish to be reunited with us or not. I have met animals who have told me that they will not choose to meet the humans in their lives after physical death."[14]

Communicator Lynn Younger says from her experience she's found that about 15 percent of animals are "able to pull off" a reincarnation—at least one that is convincing to their humans.

It would have been easy for the communicators just to give me the assurances I sought. Instead, they pushed me to look at a bigger, more profound picture. "He's moved on," Alecia said. "That's upsetting to your ego but not to your soul. It's not that he's not with you but his energy is huge and vast. He went so big I think he just didn't want to make the choice again to be in a smaller vehicle."

I see now that the most important journey I was on was the one within. What I got was not what I'd asked for but what I needed. I was led to contemplate that the essence of Brio that I loved might still really exist.

I did finally get a puppy—another black standard poodle from a breeder who'd had a dog born on Brio's birthday. I went to see that dog, but didn't connect with him. But there was a younger litter with a delightful black puppy with whom I did feel a connection. So I brought him home. But I knew somehow that this adorable little dog, whom I named Bravo, was not Brio. He had a different personality, a different energy; his own unique soul. I believe that Brio was an old soul, even as a young puppy. Bravo, on the other hand, is definitely a young soul. He lives to play and expresses his joy with a very rapidly wagging tail, which is unusual in poodles!

Something odd occurred with Bravo when we lived in the country for the first year or so of his life. I'd had a ramp off the deck built so that Brio could walk down more easily by not having to deal with steps. Bravo instantly took to the ramp; he loved nothing more than to take a running start and leap from the top of the ramp out into the yard. He did this over and over again. I couldn't help but wonder if somehow Brio was communicating with Bravo, asking him to erase all the memories I had of Brio's not being able to run and jump as he had wanted to. Maybe Bravo was expressing the release from this frustration for Brio.

As the months and years went by after Brio's passing, the reporter in me couldn't stop probing, couldn't stop looking for the evidence and explanations. I often wondered—and still do—if Brio will choose to reincarnate into this world again, or if his soul feels fulfilled enough by its experiences as Brio. I wonder too if I'll be given the chance to meet him again in my present or future lives. I do know deep down, however, that the only real truth I know about my connection to Brio lies in my consciousness of him and in our profound connection.

13
Learning to Listen

ONE DAY NOT LONG AFTER BRIO PASSED, I was driving on the highway, alone in the car. I'd been thinking of Brio and a few moments later heard clearly the sound of the metal tags on his collar clinking from the backseat, where he always rode. There was nothing else there that would have made that noise. A split second after that, the highway divided and as I was merging from the left into another lane—with my signal on—a tractor trailer barreled into my path on the right, refusing to yield. Somehow I saw it in time and slammed on the brakes, avoiding it by millimeters. I had felt strongly that Brio was with me in the car; after this miraculous near miss it seemed that perhaps he was, and that he had somehow guided me to safety.

"Oh, now I've really gone down the rabbit hole," I remarked to myself with a chuckle. But I was beginning to listen to what felt true to me. That was all that really mattered. It's not that all doubt was erased. Rather, I could see the doubt and the fear about what others would think as just feelings and not necessarily truth. I had increasingly come to feel Brio's presence in spirit myself—not only as he was channeled to me from the psychics—but as though he was walking right beside me. Or I'd feel his gaze or the touch of his muzzle in my hand.

Brio's physical presence had always grounded me. He brought me back to myself when stress and ego and all the distractions of the human world sent me spinning off into chaos. Now that he was not here in this world, I had to try to find that grounded, centered place myself. Abiding by the lessons he had taught me, I found it was not so hard. I meditated more in a very simple way. Still exploring different spiritual paths, I hadn't settled on one in particular. Anything that smacked of organized religion or a cult sent me running.

But certain spiritual teachings reeled me in. The writings of mystics like the Trappist monk Father Thomas Keating interested me. Father Thomas founded a practice of mediation and contemplation called Centering Prayer. "God's first language is Silence," Father Thomas has said. "Everything else is translation."[1] I am far from being a Catholic, but the mystics of any faith emphasize the importance of meditation, going inside and listening to "the still small voice."

In my early days of meditation that worked for me. I didn't have to sit like a contortionist or follow any rituals or say any mantras; I just tried to listen. It's not easy. Listening is a form of surrender, of forgetting human concerns and desires and the effort to control everything. I couldn't always do it. But if, in the silence, I didn't actually hear that still small voice I did begin to sense a presence within me. Even if it was only for a millisecond, it seemed like a radio signal breaking through the static of mental noise. I had experienced stillness with Brio, smelling the scents in a flower shop, breathing in the salt air on the beach. And I had felt his presence. Now I began to feel it within myself.

I continued to sense Brio sometimes, and even see an image of his face in my mind's eye. I could of course conjure that up in a conscious way, but the images that came in meditation were different. They came on their own—I wasn't consciously asking for them. They only appeared when my mind had stopped its chatter and I was at least somewhat detached from conscious thought.

I'd also become interested in metaphysical philosophy, particularly in the more mystical teachers. *Metaphysical* means "above the physical," focusing on an invisible force or spirit that governs life. Stephan Schwartz, the author and researcher who's investigated the realm of metaphysics and the paranormal, says it's not pure faith but rather data gathered from studies of telepathy, remote viewing, and prescience that should convince us that there's more to "reality" than meets the eye. "I think you come away from the research with a new paradigm," Schwartz says. "You know the old paradigm says consciousness is entirely physiological. We can only know things through our normal physiological awareness, that we are constrained by space and time. That's the materialist view. The new paradigm . . . is that our consciousness is partly physiological but partly not . . . that we are not limited by space or time."

All of this exploration was fascinating, but sometimes overwhelming. After all, what I really wanted was to be with my dog! I wanted to find "home" again. My mind wasn't going to find him for me. The animal psychics had helped me to believe that my connection endured no matter what. I just needed to be open to it and feel it for myself. The psychics planted the seeds of curiosity and belief within me; they did the groundwork. But from there, my spiritual awareness had to grow, as I personally sought Brio's otherworldly presence in my own world.

Dogs teach one to listen. They keep us in the moment, in the heartbeat and the breath of the moment. Indeed the English word *spirit* comes from the Latin *spiritus,* which means "breath." Animal communicators tell us that the key to really "hearing" one's animal is to be open and trust one's own intuition about what the animal is "saying." I have come to believe that they are right in saying that we are all born with intuition that gives us a connection to other beings. But our culture leads us to distrust it, to rely on our minds, on reason, on empirical proof.

My exploration into the world of the invisible, a world of powers we may not understand, has put me in contact with many "dog people" who speak of how they too have touched this mysterious world through relationships with their dogs—during and after physical life. Some were people I would have least expected to be open to such experiences—least of all to admitting them for public consumption! Instead, I found great generosity and willingness to be open about considering the validity of their encounters with the paranormal.

The documentary filmmaker D. A. Pennebaker spoke about such incidents in the weeks after his beloved dog Bix passed. "Penny," as Pennebaker is known, said, "I felt him with me sometimes. I woke up in the night and I thought I heard him barking. It's such a clear sound. I know it couldn't be Bix, but in a way I did think it was Bix. It happened two or three times." Penny's wife didn't wake up. To Penny, those barks in the night clearly held a reality and a power that remains with him today.

Another friend told me she'd heard the "pat-pat" of the feet of her family's Chihuahua on the sofa shortly after he'd passed. She's convinced she wasn't dreaming or in a trance or just imagining and wishing that their dog was there. She has that sense of knowing what she heard, just like others who recount similar experiences.

Border collie handler Donald McCaig, a down-to-earth sheep farmer and author, was not a person I would expect to tell of strange appearances by dogs who had passed from this Earth. Yet he did. He is also convinced that his living dogs sensed these visits as well. Recently, McCaig's collie June, who'd been an especially close and reliable partner working the sheep, became ill with lymphoma and died. In life, McCaig's communication with June had been deep.

When I asked him if he ever felt that June is around now, he answered immediately. "Oh yes, she came back two nights after she died, which is pretty common. It just happens. All the dogs are excited." As in the past, when McCaig's other dogs had died, the living animals began barking as if someone had just arrived in the house.

There are other remarkable stories of nonhuman animals who apparently sense the passing of another creature to whom they are close. When the famous conservationist Lawrence Anthony died in 2012, two herds of wild elephants traveled for twelve hours through the bush to reach his house. Anthony had rescued and rehabilitated the elephants who had been destined to be shot. When the elephants arrived at Anthony's home, there they stayed, apparently holding a vigil for two days before going back to the bush. Rabbi Leila Gal Berner commented,

"A man's heart stops, and hundreds of elephants' hearts are grieving. This man's oh-so-abundantly loving heart offered healing to these elephants, and now, they came to pay loving homage to their friend."[2]

English animal communicator Margrit Coates believes that animals are very sensitive to "spirits." "They see and sense beyond the boundaries of time and space," she says.[3]

Donald McCaig told me, "I can't prove anything." But there was no doubt in his voice. "I'm convinced," he says of his other dogs' reaction after June's death, "that she came back to make sure we're alright before she moved on, before the journey to the other side."

Numerous people testify to similar experiences. Kathy and Rick Sommer, the musicians from New Jersey who are so connected to their soul dog, Shiner, have felt his presence since he passed. They have continued to "talk" with Shiner through animal communicator Donna Lozito. In one case, Donna "quoted" Shiner as saying something to Kathy that Rick had written to her years ago in a message left on their refrigerator in Shiner's presence. No one but Kathy—and apparently Shiner—had seen that note. Nobody, including Donna, knew what was in it before she "heard" Shiner tell her.

Imagine that! It sends chills down my spine to hear stories like this—just as I felt when I heard Brio's tags jingling in the backseat of my car.

Intuitive Linda Gnat-Mullin had a client with a dog to whom she was very connected. But she shared King with her boyfriend. When the couple broke up, the boyfriend took King. Sadly, when King later died, the woman could not be there at his passing. When she later had a session with Linda Gnat-Mullin, Linda reported the great sorrow that her client expressed. "We began to feel King's presence in the room," Gnat-Mullin recounts. "You could just see the movement out of the corner of the eye." She told the client, "'He wants to jump up on the table with you.' We had the feeling—subtle but unmistakable—of the movement of the dog jumping from the floor to the table. The client began to cry. She told King how much she loved him. She was sorry she couldn't be there during that time to hold him. There was no resentment on the dog's part," Gnat-Mullin recalls—"just happiness and joy." Clearly the client as well as Gnat-Mullin absolutely believe that they felt the presence of the dog connecting from the world of Spirit.

Biologist Rupert Sheldrake has explored the experience of bereaved people who sense the presence of a loved animal after death. He's heard stories of people who've felt an animal's presence after death. "A cat, for example, sitting on a bed," he told me. "People don't often talk about it," Sheldrake adds, "because they feel they will be thought mad."

If a beloved animal exists in spirit, is that spirit part of Sheldrake's morphic fields in some arena or network of eternal consciousness and awareness? Sheldrake is cautious to say that such an idea would go "way beyond my normal hypothesis" of morphic fields linking beings in life. However, "It's possible," he adds "that if two people are connected by an elastic band one will feel it if the other drops it."

Critics point out that there are more "rational" explanations for apparent appearances of loved animals who have died. Perhaps these instances are simply "waking dreams" or hallucinations that occur in the twilight zone between sleep and wakefulness.

There is, however, research showing that it is a fairly common experience for people who have lost a loved human being to feel they have felt or heard something from that person after death. A 2001 Gallup poll showed that 54 percent of people responding believed, or were at least open to the possibility, that people can communicate mentally with those who have died.[4] A survey by the late Reverend Andrew Greeley at the National Opinion Research Center showed that 42 percent of adults who were asked if they "felt really in touch with someone who had died" answered in the affirmative.[5] Greeley noted that more American adults believed in life after death in the 1990s than in the 1970s.[6] Roper surveys show that about one-fifth of Americans believe that people who have died can communicate with the living. Only about half of Americans totally rule out the possibility that some people can communicate with the dead.[7]

Psychologist Louis LaGrand is a professor emeritus at the State University of New York and an expert on grief. He cites a growing interest in researching what is called after-death communication, or ADC. LaGrand himself has heard numerous stories about such ADC experiences, which he says involved "the senses of sight, hearing, touch, and smell as well as the intuitive faculties, sometimes referred to as our 'sixth sense.' Each story engaged my curiosity and caused me to reevaluate my beliefs about the meanings of these encounters."

LaGrand describes himself as, "at best, a hopeful skeptic," one "who has not teethed on the extraordinary, the unusual or paranormal phenomena: I have no yen for the unfamiliar, or the unknown." Yet the experience of hearing so many stories of after-death communication has changed him. He continues to have "a dutiful respect for science. It has brought us a long way—but not far enough because its method of exclusive reliance on the five senses for gathering data is constrictive to the rich evidence of subjective experience." LaGrand himself, he emphasizes, has never had an experience of after-death communication.[8]

Like Rupert Sheldrake, LaGrand has crossed over into dangerous territory for a scientist trained in the Western empirical tradition. They're looking for "evidence" that is not physically verifiable or explainable in terms of the five senses.

How do we really explain the anecdotes told by people who've had ADCs with an animal? Wishful thinking by those in grief? But then how do we explain specific "quotes" from a dog who might have heard something when he was alive and seemingly repeats it to an animal communicator? How to explain Donald McCaig's dogs barking and reacting as McCaig himself felt the presence of their departed pack member?

These are questions that surely will be answered subjectively—by scientists seeking empirical evidence in one way, by believers and those open to the spiritual and paranormal in another. Yet there are some signs of convergence between these two camps. Theories of quantum physics coincide with ideas about the oneness and interconnectedness of the universe that had been the province of spiritual thought. The principle of non-locality says that objects affect each other irrespective of distance and time. Once connected, always connected.[9] And the principle of entanglement holds that such connections are permanent.[10] So can we think that souls are entangled, connected forever?

Of one thing I am now sure: a soul is a curious thing. It cannot be seen or touched, yet it is felt more profoundly than any sensation of the five senses. When I truly feel Brio in that space within me, there is no doubt. That in itself is a gift and a lesson for which I am grateful beyond measure. I yearned to "hear" Brio, to listen to what he said. Perhaps not every dog person will be so driven in that yearning as I was. But the gifts of a real and deep human-animal connection are there for all of us if we are ready to receive them.

Even at the most basic level of interaction—that of training a dog— there are such benefits. Some say that training may break a dog's spirit. If approached in the right way, however, with consideration for this nonhuman sentient animal as a conscious, feeling being, training can be the beginning of a conversation. It does not have to be about control, as I once thought. I came to see it rather as learning a language that we both could understand. And that language of training, of "sit," "stay," "come," was only the beginning.

For me it wasn't enough. I wanted a more profound conversation. For that, it does really come down to learning to listen. One cannot approach a dog or any other animal from the position of superiority— that of a superior being who's doing all the talking. We humans have much to learn from our fellow animals; we need to recognize that. Our culture, again, does not always encourage that attitude. So we need to be gatekeepers, watching our attitude as we develop a relationship with a dog. Humility is a quality to develop. That's part of the surrender in learning to listen.

What I have come to understand is that there is an actual, curious, sometimes incomprehensible interaction with the being I love in a non-physical dimension. When one experiences the presence of an animal in spirit, there is a kind of knowing that drives out the need for empirical proof. I know now, without a shadow of a doubt, that Brio is and always will be my soul dog.

14

In Mind's Eye

I HAD COME TO SEE BRIO AS MY GUIDE. In life, he had taught me in so many ways to live in the moment, to seize the wind, to savor joy. Now in his afterlife, I continued to seek his messages—through the translators at first, then increasingly on my own. I sought that reassurance I'd always found looking into his eyes and knowing that no matter what he was there; we were together.

There were good times in the years after Brio's physical death, but there have also been times of great challenge for me—personally and professionally. I struggled to reinvent myself as the industry that had sustained my career underwent profound changes. It became harder to find work. As a freelance producer, I now had to become a fundraiser in order to support the programs I wanted to do. There were long spans when the money wasn't coming. There were legal problems. There were times of terror. I had to move, sell an apartment, sell a house, and move again. Through it all I held to Brio, to our connection, to his calm confidence and wisdom. On the darkest days, I would call my animal communicator friends and ask Brio for guidance. "Will I sell my house; will I live in poverty?"

When I connect with Brio, I come back to myself and am reminded of how to listen to my own spirit and intuition. Many of the specific messages that came via the animal psychics have proved true. There have been situations—and continue to be—that seem to be insurmountable. Some of the communicators would say that Brio could not give specific answers or predictions; he could only support me. Some, however, would tell me that, even in the face of such difficult situations, I shouldn't panic, that things would work out.

That happened with a threatening legal situation that I felt was not going to be resolved in my favor. Brio's message was that it would be okay. It actually was resolved. I myself had not believed in that outcome, even after the reassurance from Brio. So Donna Lozito, the animal communicator who relayed the information, couldn't have been reading my mind. In retrospect, I still have no explanation—except the grace of the universe, of Spirit.

There have been numerous other instances like that one. The more they occurred, the more I trusted the messages. That has been a great gift from Brio. As I came to trust him, I have also learned to trust myself more, to trust my own intuition. I look back now to that childhood experience when I lived in the Mayan era and had been to Chichén Itzá. My mother and grandmother didn't believe me; they argued me out of my own instinct. So I had learned not always to trust that guide within myself.

I know now that I'm not the only person with a soul dog who asks for guidance after a dog's passing. Kathy Sommer remembers that animal psychic Donna Lozito told her and her husband that Shiner was "here for the purpose of helping us move forward." Kathy continues to ask for specific answers from Shiner through Donna. "I'm trying to move in different aspects of my life, and he's been there to nudge and push."

Elizabeth Barrett, a retired librarian in Arizona, had a very close relationship with her German shepherd Jazmine—Jazzy—in life. She'd taken her in as a foster care provider and the bond between them, helped by animal communicator Lynn Younger, grew stronger and stronger. After Jazzy passed, it became stronger still. Elizabeth too senses Jazzy's presence. "I feel like she's in the car with me a lot,"

Elizabeth told me. "She has become one of my A-team of angels. I feel like she was a guide for me in physical life, but now she's one of them." Elizabeth says that the connection with Jazzy has allowed her to "step into my own power."

I do not always hear what I want to hear from the communicators. However, at times, such an unwanted message turned out to confirm what I actually felt myself—but had buried deep down in denial. In one instance a communicator "translated" a prediction that felt like a blow to joy and hope in a relationship. It even led me to question my bond with Brio. Would a soul mate, the being I trusted above all others, cause pain? No matter the accuracy of the message, if I couldn't believe in it was I then not to believe in my guide? There was no one but myself to go to for the answer.

And therein lay the answer and the lesson. The requirement was to rely first and foremost on that voice within myself, not to any psychic or middleman. As Donna Lozito once said of Brio, "His purpose was to root you in your own spirit, to become your own authority in your life." (Incidentally, as the years passed, that message I had initially resisted did in fact prove to be true!)

I'd been told that Brio came to me for a reason. Cindy Brody, the animal communicator and energy healer in upstate New York, agrees that the connection with a soul dog is no accident. "I find animals are really angels and they're coming to help us through the darkest parts of our lives or to teach us lessons that we haven't been successful in learning. And when dogs speak and people listen, people change their lives."

Over the years, those who had witnessed my relationship with Brio often said they had seen it was a special connection. Many of them were acquaintances and fellow dog people in the neighborhood. After Brio physically died, and as some of these neighbors and friends went through the physical death of their own dogs, some approached me for advice. How had I dealt with Brio's physical death? What had helped me? They wanted to know more about my relationship with Brio in life.

How had it become so close? I revealed my journey into the world of psychics and mediums selectively, even to my close friends. The connection between Brio and me was unique. It belonged to us and us alone. But I'd come to realize that it was not exclusive. There were others with soul dogs, others who wanted to share experiences and connect with someone about those events.

No one can tell someone else how to embark on and sustain a spiritual journey. What helped me and what proved true for me may not be true for another person. But I discovered the power of silence, that still space inside. In the quiet of the moment, that's where I could hear Brio, where I can now actually see him sometimes with that gaze—eye to eye.

I never took a course to learn about how to communicate with animals. I know that these classes help many people eager to connect more closely with their animal companions. For me it seemed more helpful—certainly at the beginning of my journey—to speak one-on-one with the animal psychics and listen to what they "heard" from Brio. It felt like a confirmation, a support, at a time when I had little trust in my own intuition.

But then there was the change. The more the communicators' words confirmed what I felt, the more I trusted my own instincts. The more they translated those messages from Brio and they were validated by events, the more I believed. I came to know that my own consciousness was truly connected—*entangled* to use that term from quantum physics—with Brio's consciousness. I'd wanted profound and lasting connection with another being and I got it—plus what I *didn't* expect. Through connection with the soul of another being, I came to know my own.

Realization comes to people in a variety of ways. For Alecia, it was the exercise practice of qigong, which is based on the Chinese concept of a life force that governs existence. Alecia recalls that "I became aware that there is an energy force that runs through everything . . . not just me but the plants, the water, the earth. I just kept feeling I was not separate from that which I was looking for." After that insight her psychic abilities increased.

For me, part of the shift in perception has been a changed view of all fellow creatures on this planet. For much of my life, I now realize, I'd drawn my perspective from those of my parents and friends and the culture at large. I'd always loved the animals I'd known and met, and even felt a special intimacy with them. But I hadn't truly known who they were, nor had I understood their profound meaning and purpose in our lives. And I also knew little about how they are treated—and often abused; I thought little about it.

Today our culture is beginning to move toward a new mind-set—a new attitude toward nonhuman sentient beings. The animal rights movement is part of this. Lawyers are bringing court cases on behalf of animals caged for years in circuses and in laboratories, or otherwise abused. Recently, for example, New Zealand and France recognized nonhuman animals as sentient beings. In the United States, sanctuaries are being established to rescue farm animals from the abuses of factory farming. The United States, however, still lags behind other nations in protecting farm animals.

My thoughts and concerns for animals are now constantly present in my life. That now includes my diet. I am not yet a vegetarian or a vegan. But like many others, I eat very little red meat. I may go further down the road to vegetarianism. These are decisions everyone must make for themselves in their own time. Alecia, for instance, still eats some meat—but with a difference. "I'm very conscious of how I eat meat; conscious of where it comes from," she says. "I say a blessing for my neighbor's cow before it goes to slaughter. I have to be aware that this was a life that was sacrificed for me and to show gratitude. In a world in which we eat animals and want a certain leather purse, how easy it is to believe that animals don't have any consciousness, that they don't care if they're killed to be my purse, which I'm going to get rid of next year anyway."

I have loved to eat bacon and ham for most of my life. Lately, however, I find that before buying or eating these treats, I think first of a huge transport truck I recently passed on the highway. It was open on the sides with wooden slats through which the snouts of pigs were poking. No doubt they were headed for slaughter. I cannot get that image out of my mind. It is a call to change my ways.

It's easier no doubt to express our love and concern for animals by buying things for them. Look at the booming industry of pet products. Numbers talk. The pet industry market size in the United States was estimated at between $69.51 and $72.13 billion in 2017. Some analyses estimate the 2018 market size at $86 billlion.[1]

The growing interest among scientists in exploring interspecies communication is no doubt fueling these efforts on behalf of other species. There is a willingness to consider that these beings have abilities and a special wisdom that are of value to us. This is something many ancient cultures and our own Native American cultures understood very well. As communicator Cindy Brody says, "People want the very best for their animals. They're reaching out to me and my colleagues—chiropractors, acupuncturists, massage therapists, and homeopathic vets for animals. There are so many people out there who consider their animals family now, not just pets. They give back tenfold. The animals are keeping us sane through a very crazy period in this world by loving us, taking care of us, keeping us joyful, making us laugh. It's pretty amazing and people are really starting to realize that at this time in history."

Brody also reiterates the deep knowledge that our animals offer—knowledge about ourselves. "I've had animals tell me what happened twenty years ago in a person's life. There's no way they could have had that information. Our animals are always watching us. They're very present. They know things beyond what we think they could know. Animals communicate in very profound ways. But one thing I am sure of is a dog is not simply a dog. A dog cuts into your life. A dog is there for a reason . . . a dog loves sometimes in ways we haven't been loved before. And they seem to know exactly what it is we need when we need it."

"Did Brio come to me for a purpose?" I once asked Alecia, still looking for understanding and confirmation of the meaning of our bond at the time.

"Brio was such an amazing being," Alecia answered. "He lived totally with his heart open. That's what his energy was. That was his greatest lesson to you. What you weren't realizing was that he was reflecting back to you the truth of who you are."

No, I wasn't realizing that. I'd come to see who Brio truly was. I viewed him with awe and deep love. Alecia remembers: "That smile you always got because you loved this dog so much and you so loved the presence of his beingness. He brought you such great joy, and he brought you great expansion."

But my understanding at first was limited. Alecia spoke these words to me some years ago. I have read them many times since. Yet it is only recently that I really feel their truth. "You did get what he was doing, that he was reflecting the truth of you back to you except you were afraid you weren't going to get it. I don't know if you weren't clear enough to really receive the lesson that dog was sharing with you. The biggest lesson of his life working with you is that within this life you *will* get that. From time to time seeds are planted and when we really embrace it and get it on a cellular level, sometimes we're lucky enough to get it within the life span of the people or animals that are sharing this with us. They're planting the seeds and they're watering them until one day it's like waking up. 'Oh, my God, on a cellular level, I completely get what was being shown. For whatever the reason, now I can embody it.'"

In other words, I now see that Brio was—and is—showing me that the awe and love I felt for him, that I saw in him, is also in myself. We are connected. We are of the same life force, the same spirit. As the great Welsh poet Dylan Thomas offered, "The force that through the green fuse drives the flower . . . the force that drives the water through the rocks drives my red blood."[2] I have come a long way. What a gift! The term *unconditional love,* the repeated statements about what dogs give us, can often go through our ears but not deep into our being, our awareness and hearts. That takes revelation. It takes time.

One of my terms of endearment to Brio, in our private conversations, was "Nobody could love you more." That capacity for love that I saw in him, and wanted to give back to him, has truly become a part of me now.

EPILOGUE

Wonderful and Secret Messages

THE JOURNEY WITH BRIO, PAST AND PRESENT, has awoken me in so many ways. My perspective has become a larger one, a more compassionate one, one that is open to possibility, to transformation, to hope for a new way of being in the world alongside our fellow beings. I hasten to add that I am no angel and surely never will be! But I know that I hold within me those seeds Brio planted, and they are sprouting.

Some would say (and some *did* say) that I had turned Brio into God. I now see that he is part of God, or Spirit. The essence of Brio was—and is—his clear and pure connection to that source. That was the power of his presence in physical life. Through him, I came to feel, at least at moments, the same connection in myself, in that core within me. I believe it lies within all beings, linking us, when we are open to it. I have now experienced enough of what cannot be explained by our five senses or empirical reasoning to know, in the deepest part of me, that this essence within endures—call it consciousness or spirit or soul.

Once when I was talking to Dawn on the phone some years after Brio had physically left this Earth, she stopped talking suddenly and remarked that a beautiful large black and gold butterfly had landed on her window screen. "It's just sitting there," she said. "They don't usually do that." The butterfly remained on the screen as we continued to talk. We both felt that perhaps it was some sign from Brio.

Silvia Rossi, the medium, had told me that sometimes people or other creatures who are close to us will use "different ways to communicate. They use what we think is a coincidence. A butterfly may come and rest on your hand or shoulder or nearby. That may be a sign. A lot of odd things may seem coincidental on our side, but a loved one is trying to reach out on their end—and because they don't have vocal cords or physical presence, they use their energy. The energy can penetrate our mind or enter a small being like a butterfly or a bird, which will manifest." I remember too that the day my father died, my mother left the hospital and was driving home alone. She told me that a butterfly had come and landed on the windshield—and stayed there.

I thought back to the day before Brio left, to the hummingbird that hovered at the door screen, to the frog that sat for a long time on the entry path to the house. I thought of the four-leaf clovers that so often appeared when I was with Brio—and the one I found on his flank just hours before he left. According to legend, those four leaves represent faith, hope, love, and luck.

When I decided to get a dog, I had not wanted to walk alone any longer. I know that even though I may not have Brio physically by my side, I am no longer walking alone. When I am most depressed and upset, Brio's image comes to me. I feel his presence. I'm reminded of a statement from the poet William Butler Yeats. He is said to have repeated a quote he himself had heard somewhere and never forgot. "Things reveal themselves passing away."[1] Brio continues to reveal himself to me.

When I now lie in my imagination on Brio's flank and hear and feel his heartbeat, the tightness around my own heart—perhaps fear or sadness or anger or guilt—eases. The clenched fist opens; I feel release, an opening up.

I'd set out on my exploration to try to connect with Brio. I became curious about this new dimension of connection and communication that I'd begun to experience. I wanted to understand it—to explain it by some means. I felt, at that time, that if I could not do that, then I could not believe in the truth of interspecies communication by some extrasensory means. I could not fully trust, then, that the messages from Brio translated by psychics and mediums were absolutely real.

And yet I could not deny the growing knowledge of my intuition and heart, the truth of Brio's spirit and his soul. In the deepest part of me, I found no argument from the world of the visible, the world of reason, and the methods of empirical science that could trump Brio. I see him running down the beach, breathing the wind of the ocean. I see him drawing four-leaf clovers and hummingbirds to his side. I see him on top of a hill, his physical form perfectly echoing the graceful arc of a tree. Brio was grace embodied.

I am content with the mysteries that lie beyond human understanding. I do know that Brio is an energy, a spirit that I was graced to know in physical form. For me he was, is, and always will be the joy and awe expressed by the fourteenth-century Persian poet Hafiz.

These lines from "Saints Bowing in the Mountains"[2] always bring Brio close.

Do you know how beautiful you are?
I think not, my dear.
For as you talk of God,
I see great parades with wildly colorful bands
Streaming from your mind and heart,
Carrying wonderful and secret messages to every
corner of this world.

HAFIZ

Notes

PROLOGUE. AN UNBROKEN BOND

1. Riding, "Picasso's Other Muse of the Dachshund Kind."
2. Darwin, *Descent of Man,* 35.

CHAPTER 1. YOUR NAME IS BRIO!

1. Brackman, "Digging Up Bones."
2. Mary Bates, "Prehistoric Puppy May Be Earliest Evidence of Pet-Human Bonding," *National Geographic,* February 27, 2018, https://news.national geographic.com/2018/02/ancient-pet-puppy-oberkassel-stone-age-dog.

CHAPTER 3. WAKE-UP CALLS

1. Kaminski, Pitch, and Tomasello, "Dogs Steal in the Dark," 385–94.
2. Andics, Gacsi, Farago, et al., "Voice Sensitive Regions," 574–78.
3. Berns, *What It's Like to Be a Dog,* 4–5.
4. Michaleen Doucleff, "How Dogs Understand What We Say." *NPR Morning Edition,* November 28, 2014, www.npr.org/sections/health-shots/2014/11/28 /367092004/how-dogs-understand-what-we-say.
5. Samhita and Gross, "'Clever Hans Phenomenon' Revisited," e27122.
6. "The Cambridge Declaration on Consciousness," http://fcmconference.org /img/CambridgeDeclarationOnConsciousness.pdf, accessed May 26, 2018; Bekoff, "Animals Are Conscious."

7. *Unlocking a Mystery: The Amazing Animal Mind,* produced, directed, and written by Elena Mannes, aired October 10, 1996, on ABC News.

CHAPTER 5. A DANCE THAT BECOMES A SONG

1. Adam Rogers, "What a Border Collie Taught a Linguist about Language," *Wired,* August 18, 2017, www.wired.com/story/what-a-border-collie-taught-a-linguist-about-language.
2. Rogers, www.wired.com/story/what-a-border-collie-taught-a-linguist-about-language.
3. Jenny Arnold, "'60 Minutes' Chases Wofford Story about Professor and His Dog," *Spartanburg Herald Journal,* February 24, 2014, www.thestate.com/living/midlands/article13839317.html.
4. Associated Press, "Poll: 67% of Pet Owners Say They 'Talk,'" USATODAY.com, December 17, 2008.
5. Boone, *Kinship with All Life,* 72.
6. Bondeson, *The Feejee Mermaid,* 1–18.

CHAPTER 6. MULTIPLE SOURCES

1. Michelle Roya Rad, "Characteristics of Highly-Sensitive People," March 5, 2012, *Huffington Post,* www.huffingtonpost.com/roya-r-rad-ma-psyd/highly-sensitve-people_b_1286508.html.
2. LeShan, *The Medium, the Mystic, and the Physicist,* 32.
3. Joseph Stromberg, "New Study Shows That Dogs Use Color Vision After All," *Smithsonian,* July 17, 2013, www.smithsonianmag.com/science-nature/new-study-shows-that-dogs-use-color-vision-after-all-13168563.
4. *Quote Investigator* (blog), https://quoteinvestigator.com/2013/09/18/intuitive-mind, accessed March 25, 2018.
5. "Albert Einstein Quotes," *Notable Quotes,* www.notable-quotes.com/e/einstein_albert.html, accessed March 25, 2018.
6. van der Post, *Lost World of the Kalahari.*
7. Rupert Sheldrake, "Why We All Have Psychic Powers: How Thought Premonitions and Telepathy Are More Common than We Think," January 6, 2012, Daily Mail, www.dailymail.co.uk/news/article-2083279/Psychic-powers-How-thought-premonitions-telepathy-common-think.html.

8. Hartston, *Things That Nobody Knows,* question no. 57.

CHAPTER 7. THE INVISIBLE CORD

1. Erickson, "Telepathy and Interspecies Communication."
2. Dutton and Williams, "Emerging Explanatory Frameworks in Animal PSI Research."
3. Dutton and Williams.
4. Dutton and Williams.
5. Dutton and Williams.
6. Sheldrake, *Dogs That Know,* ix.
7. Sheldrake, 57.
8. Sheldrake, 59.
9. Sheldrake, 38.
10. John D. Finn, "Wonder Dog's 2500-Mile Odyssey Put Silverton on the Map," *Offbeat Oregon,* January 2, 2011, http://offbeatoregon.com/index-2018.html; Friedman, *Tracking Down Oregon,* 178.
11. Sheldrake, *Dogs That Know,* 7.
12. Sheldrake, 45, 9.
13. Sheldrake, 25.
14. Sheldrake, xii.
15. Sheldrake, 136–39.
16. Sheldrake and Morgana, "Testing a Language," 601–16.
17. Sheldrake, *Dogs That Know,* 141.

CHAPTER 8. ON THE FAR SIDE

1. Coates, *Communicating with Animals,* 23.
2. "Main Topics: Quantum Theory and the Uncertainty Principle," The Physics of the Universe, www.physicsoftheuniverse.com/topics_quantum_nonlocality .html, accessed June 13, 2018.
3. Jung, *Synchronicity,* 8.
4. Sheldrake, *Dogs That Know,* 25.
5. Wohlleben, *Hidden Life of Trees,* 9–11.
6. Dreifus, "Gregory Berns Knows," D5.
7. Dreifus, D5.

8. Fouts, Fouts, and Van Cantfort, "The Infant Loulis Learns Signs," 281–82; Fouts and Fouts, "Chimpanzees' Use of Sign Language," 28.

9. Riley, "The Dolphin Who Loved Me."

10. Denise Herzing, "The Language of Dolphins: Denise Herzing at TED2013" (TED Talk presentation, February 2013), www.ted.com/talks/denise_herzing_could_we_speak_the_language_of_dolphins.

11. Herzing, www.ted.com/talks/denise_herzing_could_we_speak_the_language_of_dolphins.

12. Clark, "Fragile Partnership," A4.

13. Safina, *Beyond Words,* 355.

14. Safina, 351.

15. Gorman, "Why Is That Dog Looking At Me?"

16. Leonardo Da Vinci, *MSS. F 96Y;* David Hurwitz, "Leonardo da Vinci's Ethical Vegetarianism," https://ivu.org/history/davinci/hurwitz.html. Last updated July 19, 2002.

17. Beston, *Outermost House,* 25.

CHAPTER 9.
SOMETHING BEHIND THE EYES

1. Tanya Lewis, "Scientists Closing in on the Theory of Consciousness," *Live Science,* July 30, 2014, www.livescience.com.

2. Pilley with Hinzmann, *Chaser,* 140–53.

3. Julie Hecht, "Do Dogs Know Themselves?" *Scientific American,* August 23, 2017, https://blogs.scientificamerican.com/dog-spies/do-dogs-know-themselves.

4. Horowitz, "Smelling Themselves," 17–24.

5. Jon Hamilton, "Your Dog Remembers Every Move You Make," *NPR Morning Edition,* November 23, 2016, www.npr.org/sections/health-shots/2016/11/23/503072612/your-dog-remembers-every-move-you-make.

6. Fugazza, Pogány, and Miklósi, "Recall of Others' Actions," 3209–13.

7. Dreifus, "Gregory Berns Knows," D5.

8. Philip Low, "The Cambridge Declaration on Consciousness," July 7, 2012, http://fcmconference.org/img/CambridgeDeclarationOnConsciousness.pdf.

9. Taylor, *Ancient Egyptian Book of the Dead,* 55.

10. Allen, *Middle Egyptian,* 483–87.

11. Taylor, *Ancient Egyptian Book of the Dead,* 40; D'Auria, *Mummies and Magic,* 187.

12. Taylor, *Ancient Egyptian Book of the Dead,* 58; Faulker and Andrews, *Ancient Egyptian Book of the Dead,* 18.

13. Deussen, *Kathaka Upanishad,* 283.

14. Coleman, *Tibetan Book of the Dead;* Fremantle and Trungpa, *Tibetan Book of the Dead,* 20.

15. Preece and Fraser, "The Status of Animals," 251.

16. Allen, *Middle Egyptian;* Cohn, *Cosmos, Chaos and the World to Come,* 9.

17. Budge, *Papyrus of Ani,* 576–82.

18. Rose Dixon, "The Afterlife Hall of Judgment: 42 Questions," RoseDixon .net (blog), November 14, 2012, https://rosedixon.net/2012/11/14/the-afterlife -hall-of-judgement-42-questions.

19. Dixon, https://rosedixon.net/2012/11/14/the-afterlife-hall-of-judgement -42-questions.

20. Grant, *Winged Pharaoh,* 317.

21. Graeber, "Ancient Egyptian Animals," C21.

22. Preece and Fraser, "The Status of Animals," 248.

23. Hyland, *God's Covenant with Animals,* xii.

24. Panaman, "How to Do Animal Rights," 48.

25. Aquinas in Ryder, *Animal Revolution,* 29.

26. "Do Animals Have Souls?" https://do-animals-have-souls.info, accessed June 3, 2018.

27. Eliezer Segal, "Afterlife for Animals: Jewish Authorities Disagree as to Whether All Cows Go to Heaven," *My Jewish Learning* (blog), June 6, 2002, www.myjewishlearning.com/article/afterlife-for-animals.

28. Segal, www.myjewishlearning.com/article/afterlife-for-animals.

29. Grant, *Speaking from the Heart,* 215.

30. O'Donohue, *Mo Anam Cara,* xviii.

CHAPTER 10.
DAYS OF THE HUMMINGBIRD

1. "Hummingbird Symbology," Crystal Links: Metaphysics and Science Website, www.crystalinks.com/hummingbird.html, accessed June 16, 2018.

2. The Hummingbird Web Site, www.hummingbirdworld.com, accessed October 10, 2017.

3. Coates, *Communicating with Animals,* 173.

CHAPTER 11. OUT OF THIN AIR

1. Kathleen Weldon, "Paradise Polled: Americans and the Afterlife," *HuffPost* (blog), June, 15, 2015, www.huffingtonpost.com/kathleen-weldon/paradise -polled-americans_b_7587538.html, updated Dec. 6, 2017.

2. Marquand, "Influence of New Age."

3. See https://stephanaschwartz.com/category/video-2 and www.huffingtonpost .com/author/stephan-a-schwartz.

4. Targ and Puthoff, *Mind-Reach.*

5. Targ, Russell, and Puthoff, "Standard Remote-Viewing Protocol (Local Targets)," *CIA Library,* www.cia.gov/library/readingroom/docs/CIA-RDP96 -00788R001300050001-3.

6. Paul Mainwood, "Einstein Believed in a Theory of Spacetime that Can Help People Cope with Loss," *Forbes,* December 28, 2016, www.forbes.com/sites /quora/2016/12/28/einstein-believed-in-a-theory-of-spacetime-that-can-help -people-cope-with-loss/#4f22dd455d25.

7. "Animal Spirits," *Warpaths2peacepipes* (blog), www.warpaths2peacepipes.com /native-american-culture/animal-spirit.html, accessed October 15, 2017.

8. Sandra Ingerman, "Shamanism: Healing Individuals and the Planet," www .sandraingerman.com/abstractonshamanism.html, accessed June 16, 2018.

9. Shaman Links, www.shamanlinks.net, accessed October 15, 2017.

10. Ingerman, "Shamanism," www.sandraingerman.com/abstractonshamanism .html.

CHAPTER 12.
TO REINCARNATE OR NOT TO REINCARNATE

1. *Stanford Encyclopedia of Philosophy,* s.v. "René Descartes," https://plato.stanford .edu/entries/descartes, accessed August 29, 2017.

2. *Stanford Encyclopedia of Philosophy,* s.v. "Pythagoras," https://plato.stanford .edu/entries/pythagoras, accessed September 27, 2017.

3. Burkert, *Greek Religion,* 300–301; Copleston, *History of Philosophy,* 30–31.

4. Rachel Martin, "Searching for the Science behind Reincarnation," *NPR Weekend Edition Sunday,* January 5, 2014, www.npr.org/2014/01/05/259886077 /searching-for-science-behind-reincarnation.

5. Stevenson, *Children Who Remember Previous Lives,* 209–10.

6. Rachel Martin, "Searching for the Science behind Reincarnation," *NPR Weekend Edition Sunday,* January 5, 2014, www.npr.org/2014/01/05/259886077 /searching-for-science-behind-reincarnation.

7. Martin, www.npr.org/2014/01/05/259886077/searching-for-science-behind -reincarnation.

8. Martin, www.npr.org/2014/01/05/259886077/searching-for-science-behind -reincarnation.

9. Planck in Joseph H. Fussell, "Review and Comment"; Marian Yates, "Physicists Claim that Consciousness Lives in Quantum State After Death," Core Spirit, www.corespirit.com/physicists-claim-that-consciousness-lives-in-quantum -state-after-death, accessed May 23, 2018; Dr. Rolf Frobose, "Scientists Find Hints for the Immortality of the Soul," June 17, 2014, quoted in www .huffingtonpost.co.uk/rolf-froboese/scientists-find-hints-for-the-immortality -of-the-soul_b_5499969.html.

10. Interview with Hans-Peter Durr by Holger Fuß, "Physics and Philosophy: In the Beginning was the Quantum Spirit." *P.M. Magazin* (May 2007).

11. Brown, *Conversations on the Edge,* 65.

12. Kaiser, *Tales of an Animal Communicator,* 40–41.

13. Kaiser, 40.

14. Ortzen, "Animal Healer Has Happy Tails," 16.

CHAPTER 13. LEARNING TO LISTEN

1. Keating, *Intimacy with God,* 55.

2. "Elephants Travel 12 Hours to Attend a Vigil for the Man Who Rescued Them," *Sunny Skyz* (blog), October 12, 2016.

3. Ortzen, "Animal Healer Has Happy Tails," 16.

4. Brigid McCormick, "The Impact of Post Death Communication (PDC) on Bereavement," (master's thesis, Massey University, May 2014), https://mro .massey.ac.nz/handle/10179/6327.

5. Harpur, *There Is Life;* Krause, "Reported Contact with the Dead."

6. Greeley and Hout, "Americans' Increasing Belief," 813–35.

7. "Paradise Polled: Americans and the Afterlife," Cornell University, https:// ropercenter.cornell.edu/paradise-polled-americans-and-the-afterlife, accessed October 15, 2017.

8. LaGrand, *After Death Communication.*

9. "Science," Starstuffs, www.starstuffs.com/physcon/science.html, accessed September 1, 2017.

10. "Main Topics: Quantum Theory and the Uncertainty Principle," Physics of the Universe, www.physicsoftheuniverse.com/topics_quantum.html, accessed April 30, 2018.

CHAPTER 14. IN MIND'S EYE

1. "Pet Industry Market Size & Ownership Statistics," APPA, www.americanpet products.org/press_industrytrends.asp, accessed June 12, 2018; CISION: PR Newswire, www.prnewswire.com/news-releases/us-pet-industry-sales-reach -86-billion-growth-projected-amid-changes-finds-packaged-facts-pet-market -outlook-300612322.html, accessed June 12, 2018.

2. Thomas, "The Force That Through the Green Fuse Drives the Flower," from *The Poems of Dylan Thomas,* 90.

EPILOGUE.
WONDERFUL AND SECRET MESSAGES

1. Yeats, *Collected Works,* 297; Richard M. Weaver, "Things Reveal Themselves Passing Away, *Austin Storm* (blog), October 6, 2016.

2. Hafiz, from Daniel Ladinsky, *I Heard God Laughing,* 18.

Bibliography

Ackerly, J. R. *My Dog Tulip*. New York: New York Review of Books, 1965.

Allen, James P. *Middle Egyptian: An Introduction to the Language and Culture of Hieroglyphs*. New York: Cambridge University Press, 2000 and 2014.

Andics, Attila, Márta Gacsi, Tamás Farago, et al. "Voice Sensitive Regions in the Dog and Human Brain Are Revealed by Comparative fMRI." *Current Biology* (February 2014): 574–78.

Andrews, Kristin. *The Animal Mind: An Introduction to the Philosophy of Animal Cognition*. London and New York: Routledge, 2015.

Bekoff, Mark. "Animals Are Conscious and Should Be Treated as Such." *New Scientist* 2883 (September 22, 2012).

———. "Observations of Scent-Marking and Discriminating Self from Others by a Domestic Dog: Tales of Displaced Yellow Snow." *Behavioral Process* 55 (2001): 75–79.

Benjamin, Carol Lea, and Denise C. Wall. *Do Border Collies Dream of Sheep? Two Puppies Grow Up: One to Be a Sheepdog, the Other a Service Dog*. Hillsborough, N.J.: Outrun Press, 2011.

Berne, Rosalyn W. *When the Horses Whisper: The Wisdom of Wise and Sentient Beings*. Faber, Va.: Rainbow Ridge Books, 2013.

Berns, Gregory. *What It's Like to Be a Dog: And Other Adventures in Animal Neuroscience*. New York: Basic Books, 2017.

Beston, Henry. *The Outermost House: A Year of Life on the Great Beach of Cape Cod*. New York: Doubleday and Doran, 1928.

Bondeson, Jan. *The Feejee Mermaid and Other Essays in Natural and Unnatural History*. Ithaca, N.Y.: Cornell University Press, 1999.

155

Boone, J. Allen. *Kinship with All Life.* New York: HarperCollins, 1954.

———. *Letters to Strongheart.* New York: Prentice-Hall, 1939.

Brackman, Jane. "Digging Up Bones." *Bark* (Winter 2014): 83–86.

Brown, David Jay. *Conversations on the Edge of the Apocalypse: Contemplating the Future with Noam Chomsky, George Carlin, Deepak Chopra, Rupert Sheldrake, and Others.* New York: Palgrave Macmillan, 2005.

Budge, E. A. Wallis Sir. *The Papyrus of Ani: A reproduction in Facsimile, Edited, with Hieroglyphic Transcript, Translation, and Introduction.* London: The Medici Society, 1913.

Burkert, Walter. *Greek Religion.* Cambridge, Mass.: Harvard University Press, 1985.

Clark, Doug. "In a Fragile Partnership, Dolphins Help Catch Fish." *New York Times,* September 1, 2017.

Coates, Margrit. *Communicating with Animals: How to Tune into Them Intuitively.* London: Rider, 2012.

Cohn, Norman Rufus. *Cosmos, Chaos and the World to Come: The Ancient Roots of Apocalyptic Faith.* New Haven, Conn.: Yale University Press, 1995.

Coleman, Graham, "Editor's Introduction," in Coleman, Graham. *The Tibetan Book of the Dead: First Complete Translation.* New York: Penguin Books, 2005.

Copleston, Frederick. *A History of Philosophy 1: Greece and Rome.* First published in 1946. London and New York: Continuum, 2003.

Darwin, Charles. *The Descent of Man.* London: John Murray, 1871.

D'Auria, Sue, Peter Lacovara, and Catharine H. Roehrig. *Mummies and Magic: The Funerary Arts of Ancient Egypt.* Boston: Museum of Fine Arts, 1989.

Da Vinci, Leonardo. *MSS. F 96U.* fol 96v. Paris: Library of the Instituit de France, 1977.

Deussen, Paul. *Kathaka Upanishad in Sixty Upanishads of the Veda,* Part 1. Delhi: Motilal Banarsidassm, 1905.

Dreifus, Claudia. "Gregory Berns Knows What Your Dog is Thinking (It's Sweet)." *New York Times,* September 8, 2017.

Dutton, Diane, and Carl Williams. "Emerging Explanatory Frameworks in Animal PSI Research." *The Journal of Parapsychology* 73 (Spring–Fall 2009): 43–70.

Erickson, Deborah L., "Telepathy and Interspecies Communication: A Multidisciplinary Perspective." *Neuroquantology* 1 (2011): 145–52.

Faulkner, Raymond O., trans., and Carol Andrews, ed. *The Ancient Egyptian Book of the Dead.* Austin: University of Texas Press, 1972.

Fouts, R. S., D. H. Fouts, and T. E. Van Cantfort. "The Infant Loulis Learns Signs from Cross-Fostered Chimpanzees," in *Teaching Sign Language to Chimpanzees*, edited by R. Allen Gardner, Beatrix T. Gardner, and Thomas E. Van Cantfort. Albany: SUNY Press, 1989.

Fouts, Roger S., and Deborah H. Fouts. "Chimpanzees' Use of Sign Language," in *The Great Ape Project: Equality Beyond Humanity*, edited by Paola Cavalieri and Peter Singer. New York: St. Martin's Press, 1993.

Fremantle, Francesca, and Chögyam Trungpa, eds., *The Tibetan Book of the Dead: The Great Liberation through Hearing in the Bardo*. Boulder, Colo.: Shambhala, 2001.

Friedman, Ralph. *Tracking Down Oregon*. Portland, Ore.: Pars Publishing, 1978.

Fugazza, Claudia, Ákos Pogány, and Ádám Miklósi. "Recall of Others' Actions after Incidental Encoding Reveals Episodic-like Memory in Dogs." *Current Biology* 26 (December 5, 2016): 3209–13.

Gorman, James. "Why Is That Dog Looking At Me?" *New York Times*, September 15, 2015.

Graeber, Laurel. "Ancient Egyptian Animals Had a Place in the Afterlife. Here's Why." *New York Times*, October 1, 2017.

Grant, Joan. *Speaking from the Heart: Ethics, Reincarnation, and What It Means to Be Human*. New York: Overlook Press, 2007.

———. *Winged Pharaoh*. New York: Overlook Duckworth, Peter Mayer, 2007.

Greeley, Andrew M., and Michael Hout. "Americans' Increasing Belief in Life after Death: Religious Competition and Acculturation." *American Sociological Review* 64, no. 6 (December 1999): 813–35.

Harpur, Tom. *There Is Life after Death*. Markam, Canada: Thomas Allen Publishers, 2011.

Hartston, William. *The Things That Nobody Knows: 501 Mysteries of Life, the Universe, and Everything*. London: Atlantic Books, 2011.

Herzing, Denise L. *Dolphin Diaries: My 25 Years with Spotted Dolphins in the Bahamas*. New York: St. Martin's Press, 2011.

Horowitz, Alexandra. *Inside of a Dog: What Dogs See, Smell, and Know*. New York, Scribner, 2009.

———. "Smelling Themselves: Dogs Investigate Their Own Odours Longer When Modified in an 'Olfactory Mirror' Test." *Behavioral Processes* 143 (2017): 17–24.

Hyland, J. R. *God's Covenant with Animals*. Brooklyn, N.Y.: Lantern Books, 2000.

Ingerman, Sandra. *Soul Retrieval: Mending the Fragmented Self.* New York: Harper One, 2006.

Jung, Carl. *Synchronicity: An Acausal Connecting Principle.* Princeton, N.J.: Princeton University Press, 1973.

Kaiser, Nancy A. *Tales of an Animal Communicator: Master Teachers.* Todd, N.C.: Aronya Publishing, 2011.

Kaminski, Juliane, Andrea Pitch, and Michael Tomasello. "Dogs Steal in the Dark." *Animal Cognition* 16 (2013): 385–94.

Keating, Thomas. *Intimacy with God.* New York: Crossroads Publishing, 2009.

Krause, Neal. "Reported Contact with the Dead, Religious Involvement, and Death Anxiety in Late Life," *Review of Religious Research* 52, no. 4 (2011): 347–64.

Ladinsky, Daniel. *I Heard God Laughing: Poems of Hope and Joy.* New York, Penguin Books, 1996.

LaGrand, Louis E. *After Death Communication: Final Farewells.* St. Paul, Minn.: Llewellyn Publications, 1997.

Leary, Lani. *No One Has to Die Alone.* New York: Beyond Words, 2012.

LeShan, Lawrence. *The Medium, the Mystic, and the Physicist: Toward a General Theory of the Paranormal.* New York: Ballantine Books, 1996.

Long, William J. *How Animals Talk: And Other Pleasant Studies of Birds and Beasts.* Originally published by Harper Bros. in 1919. Rochester, Vt.: Bear & Co., 2005.

Marquand, Robert. "Influence of New Age, Megachurches Growing Among U.S. Worshippers." *Christian Science Monitor,* August 19, 1996.

Marshall Thomas, Elizabeth. *The Hidden Life of Dogs.* New York: Houghton Mifflin, 2010.

———. *The Social Life of Dogs: The Grace of Canine Company.* New York: Simon & Schuster, 2000.

Mayer, Elizabeth Lloyd. *Extraordinary Knowing: Science, Skepticism, and the Inexplicable Powers of the Human Mind.* New York: Bantam Books, 2007.

McCaig, Donald. *Eminent Dogs, Dangerous Men: Searching Through Scotland for a Border Collie.* New York: HarperCollins, 1991.

McMillan, Franklin D., with Kathryn Lance. *Unlocking the Animal Mind.* New York: Rodale, 2004.

O'Donohue, John. *Mo Anam Cara: A Book of Celtic Wisdom.* New York: Harper Perennial, 1997.

Ortzen, Tony. "Animal Healer Has Happy Tails." *Psychic News* (July 2015): 14–16.

Panaman, Roger. *How to Do Animal Rights*. Raleigh, N.C.: Lulu, 2011.

Pepperburg, Irene. *Alex & Me: How a Scientist and a Parrot Discovered a Hidden World of Animal Intelligence—and Formed a Deep Bond in the Process*. New York: HarperCollins, 2008.

Pilley, John W., with Hilary Hinzmann. *Chaser: Unlocking the Genius of the Dog Who Knows a Thousand Words*. New York: First Mariner Books, 2013.

Planck, Max. [Interview comments] *The Observer* (London), January 25, 1931. Quoted in Joseph H. Fussell, "Review and Comment," Review of Max Planck, *Where Is Science Going? The Theosophical Path* 43, no. 2 (October 1933): 198–213.

Preece, Rod, and David Fraser. "The Status of Animals in Biblical and Christian Thought: A Study in Colliding Values." *Society & Animals* 8, no. 3 (2000): 245–63.

Riding, Alan. "Picasso's Other Muse of the Dachshund Kind." *New York Times,* August 26, 2006.

Riley, Christopher. "The Dolphin Who Loved Me: The Nasa-Funded Project that Went Wrong." *The Guardian,* June 8, 2014.

Ryder, Richard D. *Animal Revolution: Changing Attitudes Towards Speciesism*. Oxford: Berg Publishers, 2000.

Safina, Carl. *Beyond Words: What Animals Think and Feel*. New York: Henry Holt and Company, 2015.

Samhita, Laasya, and Hans J. Gross. "The 'Clever Hans Phenomenon' Revisited." *Communicative & Integrative Biology* 6, no. 6 (November 1, 2013): e27122.

Severino, Elizabeth. *The Animals' Viewpoint on Dying, Death and Euthanasia*. Turnersville, N.J.: The Healing Connection, 2002.

Sheldrake, Rupert. *Dogs That Know When Their Owners Are Coming Home: And Other Unexplained Powers of Animals*. New York: Three Rivers Press, 2011.

———. *Science Set Free: 10 Paths to New Discovery*. New York: Deepak Chopra Books, 2012.

———. *Seven Experiments That Could Change the World: A Do-It-Yourself Guide to Revolutionary Science*. New York: Riverhead Books, 1995.

Sheldrake, Rupert, and A. Morgana. "Testing a Language Using Parrot for Telepathy." *Journal of Scientific Exploration* 17 (2003): 601–16.

Smith, Penelope. *Animals in Spirit: Our Faithful Companions' Transition to the Afterlife*. New York: Atria Books, 2008.

Stevenson, Ian. *Children Who Remember Previous Lives: A Question of Reincarnation.* Jefferson, N.C.: McFarland & Company, 2000.

Targ, Russell, and Harold Puthoff. *Mind-Reach: Scientists Look at Psychic Ability.* New York: Dell Publishing, 1977.

Taylor, John H., ed. *Ancient Egyptian Book of the Dead: Journey through the Afterlife.* London: British Museum Press, 2010.

Thomas, Dylan. *The Poems of Dylan Thomas.* New York: New Directions, 2003.

Thurman, Robert A. F. "Liberation upon Hearing in the Between." Audio commentary on *The Tibetan Book of the Dead.* Louisville, Colo.: Sounds True, 2005.

———. *The Tibetan Book of the Dead: The Great Book of Natural Liberation Through Understanding in the Between.* New York: Bantam Publications, 1993.

Tucker, Jim B. *Return to Life: Extraordinary Cases of Children Who Remember Past Lives.* New York: St. Martin's Press, 2013.

van der Post, Laurens. *The Lost World of the Kalahari.* New York: William Morrow and Co., 1958.

Wohlleben, Peter. *The Hidden Life of Animals: Love, Grief, and Compassion: Surprising Observations of a Hidden World.* Vancouver, Canada: Greystone Books, 2017.

———. *The Hidden Life of Trees: What They Feel, How They Communicate: Discoveries From a Secret World.* Vancouver, Canada: Greystone Books, 2015.

Yeats, William Butler. *The Collected Works of W. B. Yeats: Autobiographies, Volume III.* New York: Scribner, 1916.

Interview Credits

I OWE A GREAT DEBT OF GRATITUDE TO ALL OF THE PEOPLE who so generously gave of their time, expertise, experience, and wisdom by agreeing to be interviewed for this book. They include dog owners, animal communicators, scientists, and other experts. Many spoke with me more than once over a period of several years. This book is a product of their contributions in very significant ways. Thank you to all.

Barbara Barber, dog owner and client of Nancy Kaiser, interviewed September 2015

Elizabeth Barrett, dog owner and client of Lynn Younger, interviewed April 2017

Carol Lea Benjamin, dog trainer and author, interviewed April 2012

Cindy Brody, animal communicator, interviewed August and September 2017

Jennifer Chaitman, veterinarian, interviewed August and September 2012

Bash Dibra, dog trainer, interviewed September 2011 and September 2014

Alecia Evans, animal communicator and dog trainer, interviewed August 2011, August 2012, September 2012, and June 2015

Linda Gnat-Mullin, animal communicator, interviewed November 2016 and June 2017

Dawn E. Hayman, animal communicator, interviewed November 2009, January 2011, September 2009, November 2009, and August 2011

Richard Heckman, dog owner and client of Donna Lozito, interviewed October 2011

Nancy A. Kaiser, animal communicator, interviewed September 2015

Jane Lahr, friend of Joan Grant, interviewed October 2017

Diana Leslie, shaman, interviewed October 2017

Lisa L., dog owner, interviewed December 2016

Donna Lozito, animal communicator, interviewed August 2010 and June 2014

Donald McCaig, author and border collie trainer, interviewed November 2011 and April 2012

David Mehler, energy healer, interviewed June 2015

Lynn Moore, animal communicator, interviewed June 2017

Jim Moran, dog walker and trainer, May 2018

Alison W. Oestreicher, dog owner, interviewed July 2017

D. A. Pennebaker, dog owner and documentary filmmaker, interviewed March 2012

Silvia Rossi, psychic medium, interviewed July and September 2011

Stephan Schwartz, consciousness researcher and author, interviewed June 2014

Rupert Sheldrake, scientist and author, interviewed February 2011 and February 2013

Kathy Sommer, dog owner and client of Donna Lozito, interviewed October 2011

Elizabeth Marshall Thomas, author and dog trainer, interviewed November 2011

Robert Thurman, American Buddhist scholar and academic, professor of Indo-Tibetan studies at Columbia University, interviewed September 2017

Jim Tucker, director of the Division of Perceptual Studies, University of Virginia Health System, interviewed January 2014

Lynn Younger, animal communicator, interviewed April 2016

Index

Horse Whisperer, 51

housekeeper, conversations with Brio, 26

human consciousness, 24

hummingbirds, 100–101

hurricanes, 73–74

images, communicating with, 56, 57–58

Ingerman, Sandra, 114

inner stillness, 105

intelligence, 22, 83

interspecies communication, 78

intimacy, 17

intuition, 62, 79–80

"invisible cord," 69

Irrawaddy dolphins, 78–79

Islam, 90

Jaytee (Sheldrake case study), 66–68

Jazzy (German shepherd's presence felt
    after death), 137–38

Jesus Christ, 90

Judaism, 89–90

Jung, C. G., 75

Kaiser, Nancy, 122, 124

Kaminski, Juliane, 22

Kanzi (chimp who learned to use
    keyboard), 77

Katha Upanishad, 86

Keating, Thomas, 128

Kentucky Derby, 35

Khury, Samantha, 18–19, 28–30, 56–57,
    58

killer whales, 79

King (dog's presence felt after death),
    131–32

kittens, 65

knowingness, 80

Koch, Christof, 83

Lady (horse), 65–66

LaGrand, Louis, 133

laughing, 23

Leininger, James, 119

LeShan, Lawrence, 57

Leslie, Diana, 114–15

Lilly, John, 77

linguistics, 45

listening, 134

Long, William J., 64–65

love, 91, 142–43

Lozito, Donna, 62, 76, 125, 137

Maat, 87

magic, 45

Maitreya, 91

Maki the cat, 4

Mannes, Elena

    afterlife communication with Brio,
        109–12

    blind study, 54–63

    Brio as guide, 136–43

    Brio's crisis, 37–42

    death of mother, 27

    decision to get a dog, 4–6

    deep connection with Brio, 141–46

    early relationship with Brio, 1–4,
        11–13, 14–17

    gratitude of, 41

    loss of Brio, 96–103

    need for connection, 20

    on reincarnation, 116–26

    selection of Brio, 6–10

About the Author

ELENA MANNES IS AN AUTHOR AND AWARD-WINNING independent documentary director/writer/producer whose honors include six Emmy Awards, a George Foster Peabody Award, two Directors Guild of America Awards, and nine Cine Golden Eagle Awards.

Mannes's first book, *The Power of Music: Pioneering Discoveries in the New Science of Song,* was based on a PBS primetime special that Mannes developed and created. *The Music Instinct: Science & Song,* a two-hour program exploring recent discoveries about the power of music and its connection to the body, the brain, and the world of nature aired in 2009. It won the Grand Prix at the Pariscience International Film Festival, the BANFF Science & Technology Prize, as well as a CINE Special Jury Prize for Arts & Culture. Other programs Mannes has written, directed, and/or produced include a variety of series and specials, such as "The Amazing Animal Mind" (ABC *Turning Point*) with Diane Sawyer; the documentary film *Amazing Grace* with Bill Moyers, which won an Emmy and Directors Guild Award for directing; and "Cover-Up at Ground Zero" (ABC *Turning Point*) with Peter Jennings, which earned an Emmy for Outstanding Historical Documentary. Mannes has also produced and directed numerous programs and segments for *CBS Reports, 60 Minutes,* ABC's *Prime Time Live,* as well as the Discovery Channel (TLC).

Mannes lives in New York City with her current standard poodle, Bravo, and a cat named Kismet.

Brio and Elena, circa 2000

Bravo and Kismet

The website **www.mannesproductions.com** includes additional information about the author and her past and current projects.